LOUISIANA PURCHASE

BY THE SAME AUTHOR

HISTORY

Goodbye to Gunpowder
The Birth of the Constitution
July 4, 1776
Valley Forge
The Battle of New Orleans
Victory at Yorktown
The Great Separation
The Tide Turns
The Siege of Boston
The War in the North
The Great Conspiracy
The War with Mexico
The California Gold Rush
The French and Indian War
The War in the South
Lewis and Clark
The Panama Canal
The Spanish-American War
The Wars in Barbary

BIOGRAPHY

Elizabeth I
A Great Life in Brief

John the Great
The Times and Life of John L. Sullivan

The Gentleman from New York
A Biography of Roscoe Conkling

Sir Humphrey Gilbert
Elizabeth's Racketeer

Sir Walter Raleigh
That Damned Upstart

Marlborough
The Portrait of a Conqueror

Bonnie Prince Charlie
A Biography of the Young Pretender

LOUISIANA PURCHASE

by Donald Barr Chidsey

Illustrated

CROWN PUBLISHERS, INC., NEW YORK

Dedicated to

The National Park System,
for its One-Hundredth Anniversary, 1972

*All illustrations, except as otherwise noted, courtesy
New York Public Library Picture Collection*

Contents

	CHRONOLOGY	vi
1	THE CRUISE OF THE RATTLETRAP	1
2	A HISPANIC WHIRLWIND	11
3	THE LURE OF STRANGE LAND	20
4	A COURSE FOR CHAOS	31
5	'WAY DOWN UPON THE YAZOO RIVER	43
6	SPEAK WITH FORKED TONGUE	54
7	AN IMPROBABLE HERO	63
8	THE MAN WITH A MILLION DOLLARS	73
9	HE CAME LIKE A COMET	84
10	A TALE OF TWO TREATIES	94
11	WHAT HAPPENED TO A TRUCULENT QUAKER	102
12	HIS HEART WAS OUT-OF-DOORS	109
13	THEY LEFT BY THE BACK DOOR	117
14	BIG DEAL	128
15	ANYBODY BUT A POLITICIAN	141
16	GO WEST, MIDDLE-AGED MAN	151
17	THE PERILOUS PATH	162
18	"I GASCONADE NOT"	168
19	HE DID EVERYTHING WRONG	179
20	DEATH AT THE EDGE OF THE SWAMP	186
	NOTES	203
	BIBLIOGRAPHY	213
	INDEX	227

Chronology

1513   Ponce de Leon discovers Florida
1539–41 De Soto's expedition discovers the Mississippi
1682   LaSalle takes possession of Mississippi Valley and
        names it Louisiana
1716   Fort Rosalie (Natchez) established
1718   New Orleans founded
1755   War between France and Great Britain in America
        begins
1762   Louis XV makes over Louisiana to Charles III of
        Spain
1763   Treaty of Paris; the Floridas ceded to England
1777   France allies itself with America in Revolution
1778   Willing's raid
1779   Spain declares war on Great Britain
1780   Gálvez takes Mobile
1781   Gálvez takes Pensacola
1783   Treaty of Paris gives Floridas back to Spain
1786–87 Shays's Rebellion
1787   Wilkinson visits New Orleans

1789 March 4, new United States Constitution goes into effect

1791 Wilkinson "resumed the sword"

1792 Kentucky is made a state; insect plague ruins Louisiana indigo crop

1793 France declares war on Great Britain; Citizen Genêt to United States; cotton gin invented

1794 Battle of Fallen Timbers; slavery abolished in Haiti; Whiskey Rebellion

1795 Yazoo Act; treaty between Spain and the United States sets thirty-first parallel as northern boundary of Floridas; Treaty of San Lorenzo el Real (Pinckney's Treaty)

1796 Tennessee into Union; October 27, Spain and Great Britain declare war

1799 November 9, Bonaparte becomes First Consul of France

1800 April 30, secret treaty of St. Ildefonso cedes Louisiana back to France

1803 Louisiana Purchase

1804 May 18, Bonaparte becomes Emperor; July 11, Hamilton-Burr duel

1804–6 Lewis and Clark

1810 West Florida declares its independence; first steamboat, Pittsburgh to New Orleans

1812 Louisiana admitted to Union

1815 Battle of New Orleans

1

The Cruise of the Rattletrap

JAMES WILLING WAS ONE of the first captains of the
United States Navy. He was not a grizzled salt who had
come up through the merchant marine with a little privateering on the side. He never trod a quarterdeck. He couldn't
have shivered anybody's timbers. In fact, when he got his
commission in Philadelphia, then the capital of the country,
in 1777, he had never been to sea; and, the epaulettes firmly
in place, it was for Pittsburgh that he headed.

Lacking though he was in experience, Willing had credentials. He was a brother of Thomas Willing, the partner
of patriot-financier Robert Morris, and their banking firm
was one of the most respectable in Philadelphia. James Willing himself had not been a success in business. His brother
had sent him west just before the outbreak of the Revolution, and he had set up as a trader in the lower Mississippi
Valley, in the tiny town of Natchez, a little north of New
Orleans. He had failed to make money there, and had failed
as well to win the affection of his fellow traders, who were
chiefly of the loyalist persuasion and sure to take the side of
King George in the contest that was coming. The other

1

traders had an even more serious charge to bring against James Willing than was provided by his somewhat radical politics: they said that when he got drunk, which was often, he got nasty.

Now he was about to return to those carping men, with fire and sword.

Pittsburgh, the town situated where the Monongahela and the Allegheny rivers meet to mix and to form the Ohio, had, until a little while earlier, been known as Fort Pitt, after the Great Commoner who turned nobleman. It was booming. Already it was being called, or was calling itself, the Gateway to the West, an accurate description. The hillsides all around were thick with timber trees from which river craft could be made, and land was virtually free, while every settler had an ax. With the handful of enlisted seamen he had brought from Philadelphia, and the somewhat larger handful of adventurers he had picked up at the Forks, James Willing soon was able to supervise the construction of a stout, high-sided river boat, a sort of galley, equipped with a mast. She was duly commissioned, the first United States Navy vessel ever to be seen in western waters. They christened her, for reasons that have not survived, *Rattletrap*.

She could not be called a brig, a bark, a sloop, a schooner, and certainly not a ship, or any other vessel that was designated by its rig, for she had no rig, only one stumpy mast and a square sail that might be hoisted upon it in any manner that seemed convenient when there was a straight stretch of river and some manner of helpful breeze. "Gunboat" was perhaps the best word, for she did carry a few weapons.

Rattletrap, then, sailed from Pittsburgh January 11, 1778, having on board twenty-four enlisted men, two sergeants, and a certain "Mr. McIntyre" as second-in-command, besides Captain Willing himself.

The rumors spread ahead that this was the naval branch

of the force with which George Rogers Clark, the brilliant young Virginia brigadier of militia, was even then engaged in winning the northwest. The two men almost certainly never met or corresponded in any way, but the rumor caused consternation among those who disapproved of the new revolutionary movement, and it was to give Captain Willing a great idea.

His plan was to descend in force upon the British settlers along the lower Mississippi, on the east bank above Manchac—below Manchac both banks were Spanish—and make them declare for the new republic of the United States, or, if they wouldn't do that, at least make them sign a neutrality agreement on threat of having their plantations and stores looted and burned. In this way he hoped to foil any attempt on the part of the British to outflank the western tip of the new republic, cutting off such supplies of the badly needed gunpowder as French and Spanish friends and a few Yankee skippers were managing from time to time to trans-ship upriver from New Orleans. Hauling goods of any sort up the Mississippi was a backbreaking and time-consuming task. It had to be done by poling, warping, rowing, cordell-ing, inch by painful inch, close to the shores where the current was least strong but where, too, the danger of attack by Indians was the greatest. It was 1,950 miles from Pitts-burgh to New Orleans,[1] and a fast flatboat or keelboat could do that in four weeks. The trip in the other direction took at least four *months*. Nevertheless, some goods had been sent up, since the beginning of the war, and it was Willing's plan to clear the way and to oil the machinery for more. At the same time he could knock all hope of resistance out of the inhabitants of West Florida, which, like East Florida, was a British province; and with luck and plenty of energy he might even get that colony to join with the thirteen that had already declared for independence. It was a daring plan, but not mad.

There was in New Orleans an Irishman named Oliver

Pollock who was a friend of the rebelling colonists and who could take care of such supply problems as might originate there. He had lived for a little while in Pennsylvania and then had gone to Cuba as a trader with connections in Philadelphia. In Cuba he had met another Irishman, Alexander O'Reilly, who was a general high in the Spanish colonial establishment, the Number Two man, in fact. A priest, Father Murphy, had introduced Pollock and O'Reilly. O'Reilly had recently been created a count. He and Oliver Pollock got along famously until Pollock moved to New Orleans. Soon afterward, the proud creoles of New Orleans, "the Crescent City," which had just come under Spanish rule, threatened rebellion, and O'Reilly was sent there to restore order. He quietly and very politely imprisoned twelve of the leading residents. Five of these were sentenced to be hanged (it turned out that there was no public hangman in Louisiana, so they were shot instead), and six were to be imprisoned for life. The twelfth somehow got himself killed in an attempt to escape—or so the government said.

Meanwhile, O'Reilly [2] was having difficulty feeding his troops, who at that time numbered almost as many as the inhabitants of New Orleans itself—about four thousand; and when Pollock came to his rescue by turning over to him, at some financial risk to himself, a cargo of flour, the count was not unappreciative and saw to it that Pollock was granted certain trading privileges that could make him rich. O'Reilly had sailed back to Cuba before the outbreak of the American Revolution, but the power of his name was great, and under the new governor Oliver Pollock remained a puissant political figure. He was already commercial agent in Louisiana for Virginia, and James Willing carried with him Pollock's commission as agent too for the new United States of America.

Pollock, who could speak Spanish, would be a big help.

Willing, on the way down the Ohio and the Mississippi, more than trebled his force. His orders have been lost, but apparently he was authorized to recruit as he went along. The joiners could not have been refined, cultured gentlemen. There were not many settlers in those parts then, and the ones who signed up with Willing we must suppose were stray trappers, renegades who had tired of life among the redskins, fugitives, perhaps deserters from the army that Clark was assembling—hardly, in any event, flavorsome. What they were looking for was loot. Willing had nothing else to promise.

The land on both banks of both rivers was unmitigated wilderness, and except for the Spanish village of St. Louis near the mouth of the Missouri they could not have seen any cluster of houses, howsoever humble, between Fort Washington (Cincinnati) and Natchez.

The *Rattletrap* let go her hook just a little north of Natchez, and Willing, in accordance with his plan, paid a visit to an old acquaintance, the planter Anthony Hutchins, loyalist. It was a turbulent visit. Willing seized this and that, right and left, and was careful to strip the plantation of slaves. This took place on February 16 and 17.

Willing let out that he and the crew of the *Rattletrap* were no more than an advance guard for the overwhelming force under Brigadier General George Rogers Clark, which was on its way down the river then. The story, of course, flew ahead of him to Natchez, his next stop, where men trembled in their boots.

These residents of Natchez, before he could reach them, got together and appointed a committee, which drew up an agreement that they submitted to James Willing when his dread presence materialized.

"That we will not in any fashion take arms against the United States, nor help to supply, nor give any assistance to the enemies of the said States.

"That our person, slaves and other property of whatever description shall be left secure, and without the least molestation during our neutrality." [3]

This suited Captain Willing's purposes, and on February 21 he signed it, stipulating however that it was to apply only to those who were "resident in this District."

He had his eye rather on those who lived a little lower down, on the east bank, between Natchez and Manchac. At their places, very soon, he struck, and he was savage about it. Along Thompson Creek and along the Amite, as well as on the Mississippi itself, he stripped many a plantation. The riff-raff he had hired were not genteel about this. But then, war is always a dirty business.

Some of the planters, terrified, had themselves rowed across the river to the Spanish side with whatever of their belongings they could carry. A few of these men cried afterward that Willing and his goons had chased them there, in plain violation of international law, such as that was, and had stripped them in Spanish territory. This is not likely. Captain Willing might have been heavy-handed, but he was not unaware of the ways of the world, and he would not, at this time, have offended Spain. For one thing, he had no other place to take and dispose of his loot except New Orleans, where he could scarcely hope for a kindly reception if he had just violated upriver Spanish territory. If he did not go to New Orleans he couldn't meet Oliver Pollock, and he could not hope to pursue his plan of enlisting in or at least neutralizing West Florida. He needed the Crescent City as a headquarters. Moreover, there was the broader scene. Spain and France, as Willing knew, were allies; each was ruled by a Bourbon, first cousins; [4] and Spain, the weaker, almost certainly would do anything that France said. France even then, early in 1778, was thinking of coming to the aid of the struggling new republic, and if this happened Spain was almost sure to follow, if only because a successful war against Great Britain might get for Spain what she wanted most in all the world—a return of Gibraltar. Such a war, indeed, might even mean the return to Spain of the two Floridas, though this was a secondary hope. James Willing, in these circumstances, assuredly would not offend Spain.

What must have been the first inland battle in the history of the United States Navy took place off Manchac February 23, when *Rattletrap* seized the British armed river boat *Rebecca*. It could hardly have been much of a struggle, for there were no casualties. *Rebecca*, like sundry other small British craft, had been operating in the lower Mississippi and in Lake Pontchartrain and Lake Maurepas precisely for the purpose of preventing such vessels as *Rattletrap* from causing trouble. *Rebecca* mounted sixteen guns, most of them four-pounders, besides a few swivels, and Willing transferred some of these to the *Rattletrap*. Not only his armament, then, but his prestige was increased; and he sailed down to New Orleans with something of the air of a conquering hero.

He was received in that same spirit. Governor Gálvez permitted him to land his men and his loot and even provided them with some public buildings to use as barracks. The slaves and other articles that they had seized they sold at a public auction.

Protests flowed in from river towns and from backcountry settlements, and there was a flood of letters too from West Florida. Those who had been hit wailed that Willing was a pirate, and they clamored for the return of their illicitly confiscated goods, while those who had not been hit— the residents of eastern West Florida—wailed that Willing was a pirate, and demanded that he be nabbed instanter and clapped into jail, or perhaps hanged. Gálvez answered them all politely, soothingly, but without any committal.

Then there hove into sight, coming up from the Gulf, H.M.S. frigate *Sylph*, whose captain, one John Fergusson, demanded that all those ill-gotten gains be returned to their rightful owners and that Governor Gálvez apologize to His Majesty's subjects for the wrongs that he had done them.

Fergusson was one of those Royal Navy officers, very common at that time, who believed that all he had to do in order to win his way was raise his voice. When in doubt, was his rule, curse—at the top of your lungs.

Bernardo de Gálvez was not to be addressed in this fashion. He knew his law, and he knew his position. The son of the viceroy of Mexico, the favorite nephew and protégé of José de Gálvez, minister of the Indies, at Madrid, who, after the king, was the most powerful personage in the administration of Spanish America, he had ideas of his own about the value of Louisiana. He had no thought of assuming a merely defensive position. He wished to take West Florida back from the British, and perhaps East Florida as well, and to fortify the east bank of the Mississippi. He would have liked nothing better than a declaration of war between his own country and Great Britain, though he was much too adroit a diplomat to give cause for such a move.

Still in his twenties,[5] Gálvez had more than just political influence. He looked ahead. He knew well that the territory of which he was governor was regarded by the crown and by his uncle's office as a mere strip of wadding between New Spain—Mexico—and the rest of the colonial world. New Spain was the richest land that Old Spain owned. Louisiana was nothing, a howling wilderness. The thing for him to do, then, was sit tight. He had precious few regular troops, and those spread over many hundreds of miles of river; he could not count upon the militia of New Orleans and that vicinity, the only populated parts of Louisiana, for it was made up largely of Negroes and French creoles who still resented the presence of the dons. If he got rough with the English they could, in the event of the war that everybody expected, send a handful of frigates up the Mississippi and blast his capital to bits. But in any case, he reasoned, the English, whether in war or in peace, would be unsafe neighbors. They were a pushy lot, always annexing acreage. The Americans, on the other hand, were largely confined to the Atlantic seacoast.

A few of them might dribble through the mountain passes and infiltrate the lands along the Ohio, but it would be many, many years, as the governor saw it, before they would constitute a real menace to Louisiana, to the Mississippi Valley in general. Hence, Gálvez said no to the English.

Fergusson barked again, bowwow; but you did not treat Bernardo de Gálvez that way; and he barked right back. Soon they were having at it, hammer and tongs.

Willing had to face the fact that his plan to take West Florida could not be put into effect once the British had been warned. He settled his affairs and prepared to go home. Pollock, as expected, had been a great help, and between them they had arranged to have boatloads of war supplies shipped up the Mississippi, eventually, it was hoped, to reach Pittsburgh and the embattled eastern colonies.

Fergusson, learning to his amazement that his profanity brought him nothing, had fallen downriver, baffled. Willing faced the realization that he was never to be permitted to make a fair grab at West Florida; and, after he had disposed of his prizes and paid off his crew, he went home to Philadelphia. He went by sea; but his vessel was overtaken by a British warship, and he spent some time in jail as a prisoner of war, first at Pensacola, later in New York, until he was exchanged for a brigadier general. By that time the war of the American Revolution was virtually over.

Was Willing's trip a success? It had cost little, it had resulted in some shipments of powder, it had frightened the loyalists of Natchez and that neighborhood, and, though it had failed permanently to open the Mississippi to United States traffic, at least it had blocked Great Britain from making a flank attack by way of the west. Yet for months afterward complaints came in from remote colonists who spluttered that Willing had been no more than a bad-tempered bandit. He had sold his prizes for a good price in New Orleans. He had paid for the upriver cargoes; and though he quarreled with Oliver Pollock—sooner or later James Will-

ing quarreled with almost everybody he met—he had made
a firm strike for liberty. But he had not endeared the new
nation to the creoles of New Orleans. He and his companions
had been hailed as heroes when first they came down the
river; but they had stayed too long, and they were not beloved.

Granted that the complaints were biased, most of them
twisted by a hope that confiscated property would be returned, still it was not to be denied that the visitors from the
North had made a bad impression. To the people of New
Orleans everything up that way, up north, was Kentucky.
Everybody who came down the river was a Kentuckian, or,
as they put it, a Kaintuck. James Willing and his men were
in effect the first Kaintucks that the creoles had seen; and
they wanted no more.

2

A Hispanic Whirlwind

SOME SAY that a happy country is one (like Tibet, or Switzerland) that has a lot of geography but not much history. Yet sometimes geography *brings about* the history of a place; and such was the case in the early American West. The Mississippi, admittedly a mighty stream,[6] nowhere showed mightier than at its mouth, which, itself unchangeable, was to change the course of events in that part of the world again and again.

The earliest Spaniards, under Alvarez de Pineda, called it (but this might have been Mobile Bay) the Rio del Espiritu Santo, the River of the Holy Ghost. Hernando de Soto called it simply Rio Grande, Big River. Father Claude Allouez, the head of the LaPointe mission, the farthest west French post, had heard of it but never had seen it, and believed that it flowed south to Chesapeake Bay, which at that time was called the Sea of Virginia. Father Allouez's successor, Père Marquette (who thought that the river emptied into the Gulf of California, which was connected, at least in his mind, with the China Sea), gave it its Chippewa name, May-See-See-Bee, The Father of (Rolling) Waters.

11

The Mississippi could be called the backdoor of the United States, its postern gate. There were many entrances to the original country, to the seaboard states: there were Charleston, Baltimore, Philadelphia, New York, Boston, others. There was only one way to get to the heart of the land by water, and that was by way of the Mississippi. The British, holding Florida, which went as far west as the Big River itself, had tried to circumvent the New Orleanian control of the delta by means of a ship canal at their outpost of Manchac and the large lakes of the back country; but even this route, if it were to lead into the vast interior, called for the use of the Mississippi, and the British grip upon it was tenuous at best.

The British had not always owned East Florida and West Florida, a land that included not only the familiar peninsula but also the panhandle and the lower third of the present states of Alabama and Mississippi. After Ponce de Leon and De Soto, after the coastal voyages of Pineda, it was assumed by the rest of the world that the Gulf of Mexico "belonged" to Spain. The French did set up New Orleans and for a little while they had a fort at Biloxi, but the shore was taken to be essentially Spanish. After Louis XV ceded the territory of Louisiana to Carlos III of Spain, November 3, 1762, this hold was complete. Spain had Yucatan, Mexico, Texas, Louisiana, and West and East Florida, so that the Gulf was her pond, as she wished it.

This state of affairs did not last. Spain got into the Seven Years' War (in America called the French and Indian War) largely, it is believed, in the hope that if she won she would get back Gibraltar. She didn't win; and the victor, Great Britain, unashamedly hauled into her own fold great masses of land all over the world, including Canada and the east bank of the Mississippi—*and* both Floridas.

In the course of that war Great Britain had taken San Cristóbal de la Habana, a prestigious feat. She could not conquer all of Cuba, and she knew this, and knew too that without the rest of the island Havana was no good; but the city served as a counter, another chip, and a blue one, in the international poker game. Spain would give anything to get Havana back, for without it her already crumbling American empire was doomed to dissolution. England took the almost uninhabited wasteland of the two Floridas as her price for getting out of Cuba.

In those days the nations of Europe, after each war, tossed foreign lands back and forth across the bargaining table as though they were cookies; and this practice was at its height at the time of the treaty that settled the Seven Years' War in 1763.

The Gulf of Mexico, then, no longer was a Spanish lake.

The value of the mouth of the Mississippi was not lost on mercantile-minded Britain. The military men stationed at Pensacola eyed with avarice poor, flat, hot New Orleans, an island city situated near the east bank of the Mississippi a little over one hundred miles up from the Gulf. The garrison there was pitifully small, the militia a collection of clowns. The wooden barricades, never strong, had rotted away. The trenches were filled with refuse. There was no fort between Balize at the mouth of the river and New Orleans itself, the territorial capital—at least nothing that a ship of the line or even a frigate could not knock to pieces in a few hours. The generals at Pensacola had their plans drawn. All they needed was a go-ahead in the form of a declaration of war. In the years between the Seven Years' War and the American Revolution this signal half a dozen times seemed imminent. In 1770, for instance, Spain and Great Britain were at daggers drawn about possession of the Falkland Islands, and the commander of all the British military forces in America, General William Gage, whose headquarters was Pensacola (it was soon to be transferred to Boston), was warned to be ready for the pounce.[7] But peace, unfortunately, prevailed.

O'Reilly's successor as governor of Louisiana, the aged Luis de Unzaga y Amézaga, had been duly warned, and had duly deplored the military shortcomings of his bailiwick. Unzaga no doubt whooshed in relief when the Falkland Islands crisis passed; but there was not much else that he could do. When the government of Great Britain began to have trouble with its eastern American colonies, and it looked as though war might break out *there* instead of between Spain and England, Unzaga cautiously took sides. Clearly, he reasoned, a fresh new republic would be a better neighbor than a strong old monarchy; and when he received a letter from General Charles Lee, speaking for the Virginia committee of safety, and asking for gunpowder, blankets, and medicinal drugs, especially quinine, he was inclined to grant the request. That was in May of 1776, and hostilities along the Atlantic seaboard already had broken out. When the English governor of West Florida wrote to ask that Oliver Pollock be arrested and sent to Pensacola, Governor Unzaga refused. In fact, he turned over to Pollock the task of sending those supplies north.

No republic ever lasts long, unless it is small, like Venice, like Switzerland, Unzaga probably reasoned. Republics, unnatural organizations, tend to fall apart, as this one surely would do.

Unzaga was succeeded in January of 1777 by Bernardo de Gálvez, who held the same opinions—and did something about them.

Gálvez could be called a Southern George Rogers Clark; but this would be unfair to both men, for each was an original, a strong individualist.

Statues have been erected to Clark, one of the more romantic heroes of the American Revolution. A Virginian from King and Queen County, a brigadier of militia of that state, he had raised a force of frontiersmen in the Ohio River valley and with it had proceeded to perform a series of military miracles in what was then known as the Northwestern Territory. The British soldiery was spread thin in those parts, but so was the civilian population, and the activity of the Indians

was such that it was difficult to persuade men to leave home
even for a little while. Clark did it, somehow. Tall, handsome, a quick smiler, he could make men follow him anywhere and fight against any odds. He drove them hard,
always driving himself even harder. He covered vast distances through snow and icy swamp water, appearing, as a
good general should, where he was least expected. He took
post after post before the British had even learned that he
was on the march. It is very largely to his efforts that we
owe the sovereignty of the states of Ohio, Illinois, Indiana,
Michigan, and Wisconsin.[8]

Gálvez got letters not from General Lee, who was by
that time in disgrace, but to the same effect from the first
governor of the state of Virginia, Patrick Henry, who urged
him to send supplies by means of the Virginian agent in New
Orleans, Oliver Pollock; and this Gálvez did, though he must
have known that it would enrage the British. Gálvez also
gave a friendly greeting to Captain Willing, and permitted
him to lodge his troops and to sell his loot in New Orleans,
despite the howl of protest that rose from Pensacola.

Willing's work had spiked the downriver-pointed cannons that were Natchez, Manchac, Baton Rouge, but now
that Willing was gone these British settlements, a part of
West Florida, were filling up again. Their residents, to be
sure, had promised not to take arms against the new American republic, but many of them, hidebound loyalists, did
not consider a promise to a pirate binding; and none, after
all, had agreed to abstain from attack against *Spain*. When
war came these were the nearest British places, and they
would be the first to cause trouble; or at least, so Governor
Gálvez had to assume. They could keep him busy from the
north while an expedition from Pensacola and Mobile sailed
up the river to smash him. So he must hit them first.

Gálvez was a gentlemanly fighter. He kept up the old-
fashioned courtesies in high places that still did something
to soften the savagery of war. Young as he was when he

went to Louisiana, he had already served his country for ten years, and for several of those years he had led his own army in the wild northern parts of New Spain, fighting the Apaches, a people for whom he had great respect. He never lost his temper, never ordered barbarous punishments, and was kind to his prisoners. There was not a vindictive bone in the man's body. He tried to restrain his Indian allies and to keep them from taking scalps, at least from living persons. He was wounded many times—he believed that an officer should charge at the head of his men—but he carried on. He often sent presents of wine or fresh fruit to the enemy general, and was quick to accept a parole. Nevertheless, he saw no reason, when he heard that war had at last been declared between Spain and Great Britain, to spread word of this before he attacked. It was a legitimate, an accepted, *ruse de guerre*, and he was to use it against Baton Rouge.

This was not a big expedition, and he had employed every known device for keeping the news of its preparation from leaking upstream. As far as anybody knew, these precautions were about to pay off—when the worst hurricane in the history of Louisiana hit New Orleans. That was August 18, 1779. Within three hours all Gálvez's boats had been scattered or sunk—most of them, indeed, sunk—and his supplies were strewn everywhere.

It did not stop him. He pulled his forces together, and a few days later he started north.

He led a motley army. There were 170 regulars, veterans; 20 carabiniers; 330 recruits, untried men, recently come from Mexico and the Canaries; 60 militiamen and habitants; 80 free blacks and mulattoes; and 7 American volunteers, including Oliver Pollock himself, who acted as aide-de-camp to the governor throughout the campaign.

They took Baton Rouge and its 375 regulars in a matter of minutes, and Fort Panmure at Natchez, with 80 more regulars, immediately afterward. Losses of life were trifling.

The enemy had not been given a chance to spike his guns or to burn his supplies.

At almost the same time William Pickles, a Yankee privateer who happened to be in town, commanding the *Morris* —originally the *Rebecca* that Willing's men had taken from the British—met and took on Lake Pontchartrain the British armed vessel *West Florida,* while an ebullient Spanish volunteer, Vizente Rillieux, on the Mississippi itself, with only fourteen creoles behind him, attacked with great fury a British transport containing fifty-six German mercenaries on their way to Baton Rouge as reinforcements (they were not Hessians but Waldeckers), and captured the whole lot, besides ten or twelve sailors.

That took care of western West Florida. Seven hundred regular soldiers had arrived from Havana, reinforcements Gálvez had not seen fit to wait for; and he was off again.

In the days of Philip II the *pie de plomo*—the leaden foot—of the Spanish court was notorious, and it had become almost a tradition. This was not so with Bernardo de Gálvez. The planners in Pensacola were making their arrangements to conquer New Orleans when they learnd that their whole west flank had been destroyed. It was disconcerting. Moreover, there was no pause. The governor did not lose his balance, but kept hitting. He left a deputy in charge at Baton Rouge and dropped back down to New Orleans, where he took another fond farewell of Dona Félicité, and then he was off, by river and by sea, for Mobile.

He had no sooner turned his back, leaving only a small jailor-garrison behind, when the pesky Britishers of Natchez, who had promised not to do so, revolted. It did not take long for the men Gálvez had left to put down this revolt. The leaders were clapped into chains, and a messenger was sent to the governor to ask what should be done with them. Alexander O'Reilly would have hanged them out of hand; but Gálvez let them off with small fines and a warning.

He would have gone to Pensacola, that place being the stronger; but he had not yet got from Havana the two thousand regulars he had sent for. He had, however, received seven hundred of these, enough with which to attack Mobile.

In this attack the governor was wounded again. His body must have been a mass of scars. But he kept fighting, and soon, slashingly, he took the town. He presented its commander with a case of choice brandy, and they said graceful things to each other.

Pensacola was something else again. Gálvez went there by way of Havana, where he used his political connections to get really large army and navy support. Pensacola was a bitter, bloody struggle; but the Spaniards prevailed. All West Florida now was theirs. They even went on, again under Bernardo de Gálvez, to take the Bahamas. They might have taken back Jamaica, as they wished to do, had not peace intervened.

The British master plan had included a massive downriver surge from Canada, but this was stopped dead by the news of Gálvez's early, brilliant victories at Baton Rouge and Natchez. It would not be possible to launch such an invasion with the southern supply line cut off. Spain did not get Gibraltar back, but she did get back both East Florida and West Florida, and it was undoubtedly the work of Gálvez that caused Great Britain in 1783 to cede to the new republic not just all the land north of the Ohio and east of the Mississippi, but most of the land south of the Ohio as well. It is not too much to say that we owe to this Hispanic whirlwind our present possession of the states of Kentucky and Tennessee, Alabama and Mississippi, as well as Florida itself. The Louisiana Purchase would not have been possible without this.

The governor's own country did not fail to reward him, and when his father died, soon afterward, the son was appointed viceroy of New Spain—and he also had jurisdiction over Louisiana, Cuba, and the Floridas, which was more

than his father had known. He was ennobled. He was raised
in military rank.

At the time of his death, at the age of 38, he was entitled "Conde de Gálvez, viscount of Gálveztown, Knight
Pensioner of the Royal and Distinguished Order of Carlos
III, Commander of Bolaños in the Order of Calatrava,
Lieutenant General of the Royal Armies, Inspector General
of all the Troops in America, Captain General of the Province
of Louisiana and the two Floridas, Viceroy, Governor, and
Captain General of the Kingdom of New Spain, President of
its Royal Audiencia, Superintendent of the Royal Estate and
the Division of Tobacco, Judge Conservator of the Latter,
President of its Junta, and Subdelegate General of the Revenue of the Mails in this Kingdom." [9]

The *French* allies of the new United States have been
honored in many ways—Lafayette, Rochambeau, De Grasse
—but no statues have been raised to commemorate the work
of Bernardo de Gálvez. There should be.

3

The Lure of Strange Land

THEY CAME POURING THROUGH the Cumberland Gap,[10] men with the West in their eyes; they came clumping across the Finger Lakes country of New York, to skirt Presque Isle [11] and plunge into the heart of the Ohio country; they slogged across Braddock's Road or, a little farther north, Forbes's Road, to reach Fort Pitt, where they could build rafts and flatboats on which to float down the river.

It was a mass migration difficult to account for. No one pursued these men. They had not been exiled from the East. Religious intolerance had not caused them to seek out new homes, nor had they been budged by economic pressure. Some moved to the sunset side of the mountains for the same reasons that had prompted their ancestors to cross the sea: they simply couldn't get along at home, or they were fleeing from their creditors or from officers of the law. Most of them, probably, did not know why they shifted. They had not been the victims of crowded conditions, for there was yet plenty of land to be developed in the east. Still, they took up their axes and their guns, their pigs and cows, their bags of seed, their shovels—sometimes, too, their wives—and they went west.

THEY CAME POURING THROUGH THE CUMBERLAND GAP TO THE
VALLEY OF THE MISSISSIPPI.

Where did that creek run? What did the other side of
that hill look like? On they went . . . and on . . .

They carried the frontier with them. For the most part
they had been westerners even while they were still in the
east, for they had lived on the outer fringe of civilization,
and could be called mountain men. As such, they favored
the newfangled rifle over the commoner musket. The distinc-
tion was important. The musket, augmented by the bayonet,
was a military weapon. Smoothbored, it was short, light,
swiftly reloaded, inexpensive, and inaccurate. A musket
might carry one hundred yards, but if it hit anything at that
distance, or even half of that distance, this was by luck. The

musket ball wobbled wildly as it went through the air, dropping to earth, soon enough, with no more force than a tossed pebble. The rifle ball spun. It went straighter and much farther. It went faster, too.

The rifle was a long and heavy weapon, clumsy to carry, difficult to keep clean, and it could not be reloaded as swiftly as could the musket, a consideration on the battlefield, though not necessarily in the forest. The rifle came to be associated with the West and with westerners. It even came to be called the Kentucky rifle, though it had been invented, and most of them were made, in Pennsylvania.

The rifle was more than John Buckskin's means of livelihood. It was his principal means of recreation as well. He and his fellows were to live isolated lives; but when they did get together for a little while, once or twice a year, a shooting match was sure to result. Blasting a tin cupful of whiskey off a companion's head was a common practice among these uncouth men, who probably never had heard of William Tell, or Robin Hood either, or William of Cloudisley. Not often did they practice at driving a nail into a tree at ten paces, but this was only because metal nails were scarce on the frontier: the boats that soon were to start their lumbering way down the Ohio from Pittsburgh were held together with trunnels, usually ash. "Fanning" the flame of a candle at fifty feet without putting it out was considered child's play. A popular sport was "barking" a squirrel. This consisted of knocking the animal off a branch, *unhit*, by shooting the bark from beneath its feet.

The frontiersman loved his rifle and cared for it tenderly. Not infrequently, like a medieval knight with his falchion, he gave it a name. Davy Crockett's rifle, the one he had carried over the mountains, the one he was still swinging when cut down at the Alamo, was named Betsy. Daniel Boone had been onomatopoeically inspired when he named his rifle Old Tick-Licker.

This Boone was a loner. Friendly enough, to meet him,

DANIEL BOONE WITH HIS RIFLE, OLD TRICK-LICKER

he really was happy only when he was by himself. He was a hunter, and a good one. He had lived with the Miami for a little while, a prisoner, but he had no love for the Indians, no notable hatred either. He killed them only when he had to. Among his fellow hunters, by whom he was greatly respected, he was known as an oddball. For example, he never wore a coonskin cap with the tail hanging down behind, as all the others did, almost like a uniform. He complained that it tickled; and he wore a floppy black felt instead.

The deeper he was in the wilderness, the farther off from other men, the more he liked it. From North Carolina originally, one of the first travelers down the Wilderness Trail, which he helped to blaze, in 1799 he was to find even Kentucky too thickly populated for his taste, and he moved across the Father of Waters to the Big Muddy, the Missouri, a point about twenty-five miles north of St. Charles, the westernmost outpost until that time. It was there that Lewis and Clark, at the beginning of their famous trip, stopped to pass the time of day with him. He was still hunting, still trapping. In 1814, when he was eighty years old, he reached the Yellowstone, all alone. But he got back safely to the camp on the Missouri, where he died September 26, 1820, at the age of eighty-six.

Boone had crossed the Alleghenies even before the war had broken out, but there were few who did that. However, when war came close, and when at last, after Lexington and Concord, there was real shooting, then an early rush to the West did begin. It was to be as nothing compared with the later push, but it was a hegira for its time. The motives of *these* men were plain enough. They were loyalists who no longer dared to open their mouths in defense of the patriots' villain, King George. Their property was about to be confiscated because of their political opinions, and they sold whatever they owned and couldn't carry, and moved away, thankful for retaining a whole skin. It was families such as these that populated the lower Mississippi Valley in the neighborhood of the Yazoo—Baton Rouge, Manchac, Natchez. There were not enough of them to constitute a real menace, though from time to time they could be troublesome.

This was a small wave, and homogeneous. During the Revolution itself there was little or no westward movement. After it was over, however, the real surge began. It was then that the pioneers appeared in droves, in swarms.

Just at first they avoided the New York State hookaround. The Iroquois still were an uncertain element. Moreover, the Indians farther west, north of the Ohio, were kept jiggling with malice by the British military commanders, who, despite the terms of the peace treaty—they pointed out that the Americans were not living up to that treaty either—kept control of scattered strongpoints like Michilimackinac and Detroit. Southerners had favored the Wilderness Road, through the Gap, and this was still the best way for many who sought to go to Kentucky or Tennessee; but increasing numbers of the pioneers were making their way to Pittsburgh, the Gateway of the West. After that, in small groups, often only one family at a time, they went by slow-floating river craft.

The boats were of various sorts and various designs—anything that would float would do—but they fell into three general classes.

The rafts were just that, square or rectangular, sometimes with a stump mast but most of them dependent upon the current in the middle of the stream, with no sort of steering device, and equipped with poles only so that islands could be staved off, or the shore at curves. Tents were erected on them as sleeping quarters, and the cargo was lashed to the deck.

A raft that had some sort of rail or sides, even if only eighteen inches high, was a barge or a flatboat. These were sometimes rowed, though they too depended in large part on the current of midstream, which often was very strong.

A WELL-OUTFITTED LOG RAFT ON THE MISSISSIPPI. From *Down the Great River*, 1887. *Courtesy, Saint Louis Mercantile Library Association*

A flatboat that had a keel was called a keelboat, and the keelboats were the aristocrats of the rivers. They could be rowed *or* poled, and most of them had masts and spread square sails when the wind was right. They were more or less pointed, fore and aft, resembling a fat ark rather than just another raft. Moreover, many keelboats had long and very wide steering oars in the stern, and these were known as broadhorns. The keelboats were bigger, stronger craft than the flatboats, and in the early days, when boatmen were concerned only with getting to some favorable settling-down site, and not at all with goods, there were not many of them; but they increased in number and in size as trade was opened with Natchez, New Orleans, and other lower-river points.

A RAFT THAT HAD SOME SORT OF RAIL OR SIDES WAS A BARGE OR A FLATBOAT. *Courtesy, Saint Louis Public Library*

The keelboats were the aristocrats of the rivers. *Courtesy, Jefferson National Expansion Memorial, National Park Service.*

The flatboats and rafts could be broken up when a home site was selected, and their timbers used to make furniture for the cabin, which itself consisted of logs. If they went far down the rivers they might be simply thrown away, after being unloaded, or they might be sold for a few dollars apiece for their timbers. The keelboat, on the other hand, if its *patroon* could find enough men for the toilsome task, might be worked upstream again, perhaps all the way back to Fort Pitt, where it would become available for another voyage.

The keelboats could be elaborate, their cabins occasionally decked out with window curtains and containing brick hearths, woodburning fireplaces. There was nothing like that on the flatboats and the rafts.

In 1813 a barge, by going night and day, made the 1,100 miles from the Falls of the Ohio (Louisville) to Natchez in fourteen days, five hours, an all-time record. Few even tried to maintain such a schedule. It was customary, rather, to tie up for the night somewhere against a shore, or to anchor a short distance out, posting sentries to guard against a visit by Indians or (what was worse) river pirates.

And so they came on, and on, those men with the West in their eyes. They responded to the lure of strange land. It was there, so it must be tamed, it must be settled. Scarcely pausing to look around, they went to work with their axes.[12]

The war had lasted nine bitter years, longer than anybody had expected, and the rebels' best source of revenue—the confiscation of Tory estates—had long since given out. The Continental paper money was despised: "shin plasters" men called the bills, even the tens, even the twenties; the expression "I don't give a Continental" originated at this time. But there was land. Land had made the nobleman noble; it might have the same effect upon the commoner, if there was enough of it. There was always land, though it might be found necessary to take some of it from the Indians, despite the first good intentions of the federal government.

Soldiers, and especially officers, were paid off with land. In order even to glimpse this property, which was of course transmontane, they had to travel far. If they sold it, as so many did, sight unseen, then those who bought the land yearned for a look at it, or else those whom *they* sold it *to*. This could help to explain the tidal-wave-like push of the middle 1780s. But there was more. There had to be. There was the land hunger, a national characteristic already formed when the nation came into being.

So they went west. They knew that they were going into a life of hardship and backbreaking toil, of peril, anxiety, discomfort, and loneliness. Nevertheless, they went.

CHAPTER

4

A Course for Chaos

DECLARING INDEPENDENCE and framing a constitution had come to be something of a habit with Americans, and they no sooner got west of the mountains than they proliferated with a bewildering rapidity into separate states. They felt that they needed a government that was a part of them, one that was aware of them and of their troubles, as the governments they had left were not. Tennessee was a part of North Carolina, and Kentucky was a part of Virginia, at first; and so it was, too, with most of the territory north of the Ohio; but that was only on paper. In fact the pioneers had good reason to believe that their nominal governing bodies, so far away, no longer were interested in them. Therefore they formed their own. It was easy. The thirteen original colonies had shown the way.

One break-off, West Florida, was to start the announcement of its separation from its mother country with: "For a people to be free it is sufficient that they will it." Spain, as it happened, did not agree.

Not all the eastern states looked with approval upon the separation movements, either. The governors of North

Carolina and Virginia in a joint resolution blasted the newly formed commonwealth of Transylvania as "an infamous Company of Land Pyrates." This objection, and others like it, probably were inspired by eastern land speculators, who were legion, and who feared for their investments in the West.

Nevertheless the movement spread. There were Franklin, originally Frank*land*, whose first governor was that debonair Indian fighter of Huguenot descent, John ("Nollichucky Jack") Sevier, who had fourteen children, some of them legitimate, and who, when Tennessee at last was made a state, was elected its governor *seven* times; Holston, named after the river, and including a sizable chunk of what is now southwest Virginia and northeast Tennessee; Wantagh, more of a defensive alliance against the Indians, perhaps, than a really separate state, but it *thought of itself* as a state; and Valdalia, and Westsylvania, and others.

"The men of the Mississippi Valley compelled the men of the East to think in American terms instead of European. They dragged a new nation on in a new course." This was written by a respectable authority,[13] yet there may be some who think it a whit too strong. True, there were westerners who looked upon those they had left behind just the way the prewar smoldering colonists had looked upon the English at home—as effete, self-seeking, shortsighted men with no thought but the making of money. Yet discontentment and a distrust of the central authority were by no means emotions confined to the West. The first two rebellions came early, and they took place in eastern states.

Shays's, to be sure, started in and was confined to the *western* part of Massachusetts, but there was nothing secessionistic about it. A popular rural movement, it made protest against state taxes and state usages and never was national in scope. It was readily put down.

The Whiskey Insurrection took place in the four *westernmost* counties of Pennsylvania. Whiskey there, as in western Virginia and the western part of North Carolina, was a way of life. It was also currency. They had no cash in those parts. They used whiskey.

In Colonial times, and especially in the New England colonies, it had been rum. Rum was everywhere along the coast. There were forty distilleries in Boston turning out nothing else, twenty-one in Hartford, and eight in Newport. Yankee skippers used it for cash when they went to the Guinea coast of Africa to buy slaves. More, it was considered a necessity rather than a luxury. The laborer needed it, it was believed, in order to keep up his strength. No farm worker would think of going out into the fields unless he knew that there was a jug of rum near at hand, and this, which was free, was taken for granted by his employer. It was acknowledged that rum could be misused, but it was accepted that it was a requisite and that life without it was unthinkable. Rum was rationed to the soldiers of the Continental Army regularly.

Whiskey, the secret of which came from Scotland, or possibly from northern Ireland—the word is believed to be a corruption of the Gaelic *usquebaugh,* literally "water of life"—appeared along the original frontier of America, the hill country of Pennsylvania, Maryland, Virginia, North Carolina. Every cabin there had its still, using rye and barley, and later Indian corn. It was the mountaineers' money, their only means of buying supplies from the seaboard settlements, for they were desperately poor. As with New England and its rum, these places took whiskey for granted. Every raft that floated on the Ohio or the Mississippi, every keelboat and flatboat, and, in time, every steamboat, carried on deck an open barrel of Monongahela, from which the crew drank, using a tin dipper, whenever it pleased them. What else *could* they drink? They were far from cows or goats that could give milk. There was no wine, no beer, or soda pop. The river water was gritty; even if it was treated with corn meal for the purpose of precipitating the mud it tasted tart, so that Mark Twain, a river man if ever there was one, was to attest that it wasn't good for anything except maybe baptizing—and not *very* good for that. Tea was unknown. Coffee, when it existed, was not really coffee but only a fiendish concoction of evans'-root and dried peapods. Whiskey was what a man drank. In most places in the West it cost twenty-five cents a gallon.

A higher price was set upon it in the East—another reason it served so well as currency. The Continental Army had paid forty cents, sometimes fifty cents, for honest-to-goodness Monongahela. They paid forty cents for a bushel of rye, a price that stayed steady even after the war.

There was, too, the matter of transportation, important to those who lived in faraway places. A horse could carry only four bushels of rye at a time, for a long distance, but it could carry two eight-gallon kegs of whiskey. Roughly it took one and one-half bushels of the cereal to make a gallon of the beverage. The advantage to the mountaineer was evident.

The fervent fluid from the mountains was to trouble the new government of the United States early in its existence. In George Washington's first administration his secretary of the treasury, Alexander Hamilton, persuaded him, and, through him, Congress, to put a tax on all whiskey manufactured in the nation. It would range from nine cents to twenty-two cents a gallon, depending upon local conditions and how far the whiskey had to be sent for sale.

Dr. Johnson had recently defined "excise" as "A hateful tax levied upon commodities, and adjudged not by the common judges of property, but wretches hired by those to whom the excise is paid." Much the same spirit prevailed in America.

The westerners were furious. How could they pay a tax when they had no money? A few revenue collectors, venturing into western Pennsylvania, were roughly handled; and at least one was treated to a dose of tar and feathers.

The westerners were furious over the whiskey tax. At least one federal tax collector was treated to a dose of tar and feathers.

Hamilton was up in arms, promptly. Here was rebellion. It must be put down. He laid his plan—he always had a plan ready—before the President.

Washington wavered, hoping to consult some of his governmental associates. But the attorney general was not available, and neither was the secretary of state, Thomas Jefferson, who was vacationing at Monticello. It was mid-summer. The only other cabinet member, Henry Knox, the secretary of war, had just resigned.

Hamilton was not abashed. He proposed that he act as temporary secretary of war. Backed by Washington's prestige, he would raise a large force of militia and with this bring the defiant mountaineers to heel. Washington sighed, and acceded.

Hamilton always had been avid of military glory, and he had suffered through the late war as a staff man, the sort of work that was suited to his talents but did not bring acclaim. To give him credit, however, he could scarcely have been seeking honors in the field on this occasion. His aim was elsewhere. He foresaw the need for an early showdown between the states—which were acting as though they were independent [14]—and the federal government, which was not yet sure of itself. Hamilton was a dedicated federalist. Why not seize this opportunity to show the states where the real strength lay? The action would be unpopular; but Hamilton, who never held an elective office and never meant to, scorned popularity, the praise of the unwashed.[15]

He raised nine thousand foot soldiers and three thousand cavalrymen, all militia, all undisciplined, and poorly trained; and with much fanfare he set forth upon his mission. For reasons that are obscure this was called the Watermelon Army, and there was more than a touch of *opera buffa* about the business.

In their march to the offending counties the members of this rabble committed all sorts of civil offenses, confirming the people of the towns they passed through in their distaste of soldiers. They were much more unruly than the little group of willful men they had set out to punish.

It was like using a sledge hammer to swat a fly—and missing.

The whole matter had been settled, on the spot, by a handful of government agents. By the time the Watermelon Army arrived on the scene the Whiskey Insurrection already was a thing of the past, and the excise principle had been accepted.

The show had cost the federal government $1,500,000 —a stupendous sum. Hamilton had estimated that his tax would raise $826,000 a year. In fact it raised less than half that. Yet it was retained. It is still in force, though it has been increased.

The picture of American diplomats as bumbling amateurs to be wound around the fingers of slick, sly, designing European experts is preposterous, but it has always been with us. The truth was and is that Yankee horse dealers sent abroad customarily got what they went for, and sometimes a little more. Their manners might not have been as silken as those of the chancellery veterans, but in the long run they were at least as effective. The tradition started early, but so did the trickery. In the very first treaty that Americans negotiated, the treaty of peace with Great Britain that ended the war of the American Revolution in 1783, there was a secret clause.

This provided that if Britain was able to retain West Florida, as she still hoped to do when she undertook to make peace with Spain, the new United States would support her claim that the northern boundary of that province should be 31 degrees of north latitude; but if Great Britain *didn't* retain West Florida, then the United States was to stand for a northern boundary of 32 degrees 30 minutes. These lines were, respectively, the present boundary between Mississippi and the southern parishes of Louisiana, and a line approximately through the mouth of the Yazoo River, near where the city of Vicksburg stands today. The strip of territory that could be in dispute was one hundred miles wide and extended from the Father of Waters to the Appalachian Mountains.

Great Britain did not get this land. When a treaty was framed the two parties accepted the principle of *uti possidetis*—which is to say, "Keep your swag"—and Spain, thanks to Bernardo de Gálvez, retained both West and East Florida.

Secret treaty clauses seldom remained secret for long, though the diplomatists determinedly employed them for many years, and this one soon became public. Spain, understandably, did not like it.

Spain was in a touchy spot anyway. A little while ago she had owned or had claimed to own half the world— Mexico and Central America; all South America excepting Brazil; the Canaries, the Azores, the Philippines, and virtually all the other islands in the Pacific, even (and this was specified by the Spanish court) those that had not yet been discovered. The loss of this, bit by shaky bit, and the success of the American Revolution, though Spain participated in it, dismayed a nation that was rooted in the belief of the divine right of kings. It had come to be the custom to chip away at Spain, a tottering giant. *"Désormais, il n'y a plus de Pyrénées!"* Louis XIV of France had cried to his grandson, the Duc d'Anjou, on his being proclaimed the monarch of Spain. But the Sun King was like that, given to hyperbole. It seemed to him that, with a Bourbon on each throne, Gaul and Iberia would have no trouble controlling the western world. A little later, and after the other countries had exhausted themselves in an attempt to make this impossible, the two did indeed regularize their "union" with an agreement known as the Family Compact, an agreement that was to have a great influence upon the fate of the new United States of America.

The French interpreted the Family Compact to mean that Spain should assist France in war any time France so commanded. The Spaniards did not look upon it this way. They had been inveigled into the American Revolution by France largely because of their desire to get Gibraltar back; and in this they had failed. The Falkland Islands incident, too, rankled. Spain had of course claimed title to the Falklands, as she claimed "all the isles and continents of the sea," and when the English began to settle there Spain told them to get out. The English did not move. The Spaniards made growling warlike sounds, assuming that their cousins and partners the French would come at a trot. The French did not move; and there was nothing for weak Spain to do but back away, red-faced. She never forgave France.

The Family Compact, then, might be assumed to be defunct; and when the Spanish ambassador to the United States arrived in Philadelphia it was with a blustery air of defensiveness. He was Diego de Gardoqui, and he made it immediately clear that in spite of the secret clause in the American-British peace treaty His Catholic Majesty Carlos III was inclined to grant the new republic one of two favors requested—but not both. The person Gardoqui addressed was John Jay, secretary of foreign affairs under the Articles of Confederation government. They knew one another, these two. Jay had been the American ambassador to Spain for almost two years prior to this time.

America could have a free port in Spain, something the New England merchants had been clamoring for, Gardoqui stated, but any plan for the opening of the Mississippi River at its mouth would not even be considered, *and* Americans must agree not to demand it.

There was a non-secret clause in the British-American treaty that read: "The Navigation of the River Mississippi, from its source to the Ocean shall for ever remain free and open to the Subjects of Great Britain and the Citizens of the

United States." What either signatory hoped to gain by this it is impossible to see. *They* didn't control the mouth of the river. Spain did.

What Spain hoped to get by threatening to close this river is another thing that is not clear, unless she was just tired of being pushed around and had decided to assert herself to the weakest of the nations with which she was confronted, the United States of America. There might be more to follow, if this worked.

Jay was a New Yorker, every inch an easterner, but he must have been warned that any such agreement would raise a storm in the West. He argued with Gardoqui. He dickered. He got nowhere, for a whole year.

Giving up, and with mercantile pressure upon him all the while to arrange for that free port, at last he recommended to Congress that the demands of the dons be met. He tried to soften this by putting a limit on the closure of the river—this much he had managed to dig out of the grudging Gardoqui—a limit of twenty-five years.

Twenty-five years was time enough, and more than enough, to stifle all trade and business enterprise throughout the whole of the West, as westerners immediately and shrilly pointed out, being joined, inevitably, by the land speculators who had invested in western acreage. The uproar was deafening. Nobody had known, until this time, that Americans could make so much noise.

Nor were all those who screamed red-eyed radicals. Benjamin Franklin, for instance, openly sympathized with the westerners. "A neighbor might as well ask me to sell my street door," was the way he put it.[16]

The Amis case intensified all this. Thomas Amis, a North Carolina merchant, had dropped down the Mississippi with a barge filled with pots and pans that he hoped to sell in New Orleans. He never got there. The Spaniards seized his craft and his cargo and turned him loose after a while to make his way back as best he could overland. This might have gone unnoticed or almost unnoticed in ordinary times. Coming as it did just after Secretary Jay had asked the Continental Congress to agree that Spain might shut the mouth of the Mississippi for twenty-five years, it raised a stink. The shops of some stray Spanish traders in Vincennes, Ohio, were raided, and their goods taken. Funds were raised, troops enlisted, resolutions passed at mass meetings. George Rogers Clark, chafing with impatience at the peace imposed upon him, and not knowing what to do with the 8,049 choice acres in the center of what is now Indiana given him by the state of Virginia for his war services, eagerly offered to raise an army and take New Orleans by storm; and he was cheered to the echo.

Such was the hubbub that the startled Mr. Jay withdrew his request to Congress.

Then the New England states raised their own howl of protest. If *they* weren't to be protected, if their legitimate commercial requests were to be turned down at the behest of a pack of uncouth backwoodsmen who didn't have anything *to* protect, then why should they, the New Englanders, play along with a Congress that could seem to think of nothing but to throttle already established trade?

The westerners were saying the same thing, of course, though their grammar was not as good.

The nation, so small, so weak, scarcely able to toddle, was wobbling toward anarchy.

George Washington was to save it, for a second time.

Washington had faith in the West. He also had money there. He owned huge tracts of land in what was then thought of as western Virginia. Some of this he had purchased on speculation; some had been granted by Congress as a reward for his leadership in the war. For a long time he had been interested in plans to open this country to immigration, preferably by means of a canal or canals. Even before he resigned his commission he had made a long exploratory trip through the Mohawk Valley of upstate New York, the route later picked for the Erie Canal, later still for the New York Central Railroad, but he believed that his original idea, for a canal connecting the headwaters of the Potomac and the Ohio, would be better; and he began to promote this idea at the same time that he returned home.

In order even to start such a canal at the logical place, the Virginia end, it would be necessary to get the states of Virginia and Maryland together for an agreement concerning building plans and tariffs. Soon Pennsylvania would have to be dealt with, and since a part of the grandiose overall plan was to build a feeder canal between Delaware Bay and Chesapeake Bay, the new state of Delaware must be included as well. That was four states: why not ask in the others, and make a real convention of it, with all thirteen? With Washington's blessing, and as a result of his inspiration (the preliminary get-together, between Virginia and Maryland, was held at Mount Vernon itself), something like this was done. The convention was held in Annapolis, September 11, 1786. Only five states—Virginia, New Jersey, Pennsylvania, Delaware, and New York—were represented, and for this reason the convention decided that it could not do what it had been summoned to do. It did, however, adopt a resolution, submitted by Alexander Hamilton, calling upon all the states to gather together and adopt a uniform commercial system. This led directly and immediately to a thirteen-state convention that was held in Philadelphia, beginning in May of the following year, and that framed the Constitution of the United States.

The West all this while, in varying pitches of anger, was threatening to pull out of the Union; and so was New England.

5

'Way Down upon the Yazoo River

Squatter sovereignty was a new concept in the Mississippi Valley, but absentee ownership and the frenzied finance that can result from sight-unseen real estate speculation were not. Wars are expensive, as kings should learn, and when Louis XIV, *le Roi Soleil*, at last lumbered into his grave it was found that the conflicts he had so cheerfully churned up in Europe, together with the mass armies called upon to implement these, had left France with no money and a mountain of debts. The new king, Louis XV, great-grandson of the deceased, was a minor, and the regent, his uncle, the Duc d'Orléans, knew nothing about money except how to throw it away.

At this moment there appeared on the scene a tall, dark, cadaverous Scot named John Law, who came out of the nowhere promising marvels. The regent, desperate, listened.

Law was persuasive, his plan simplicity itself. France beyond question owned the vast territory of Louisiana in the New World, millions of acres of undeveloped land, most of which had never even been traversed by wandering bands of savages. Everybody knew, John Law pointed out, that this land was rich in precious minerals. Just *how* everybody knew this he did not say, nor did the regent ask. The regent, sitting on the edge of his chair by this time, simply waved in signal for his petitioner to go on.

The Compagnie d'Occident, as it was originally called, was incorporated in 1717 with a capital of 100,000,000 livres. Two hundred thousand shares of stock were issued, an issue that was oversubscribed.

The company was granted a monopoly of all Mississippi River trade for twenty-five years. It had many other privileges and rights. It could mine; it could plant; it could settle cities, and even coin its own money.

The year after that, 1718, the company's name was changed to the Banque Royale; and the king himself, through his uncle, personally guaranteed its obligations. John Law was made comptroller general of the finances, a personage who rode through the streets in a coach-and-four and was huzzahed like royalty.

The rush was on. France went mad. The price of shares of the Banque Royale skyrocketed. All other prices skyrocketed as well, those for food in Paris being *quadrupled* within a few months. Rich men who wished to be richer left their châteaux and poured into the capital, cash in their trembling hands, prayers on their lips. Scores of thousands swelled the city, so that even dukes were glad to get a garret—and pay for it through the nose—that would enable them to live within money-tossing distance of the Bourse.

The year after *that*, 1719, the company was authorized to attach to itself a subsidiary, the Compagnie des Indes, which was given the exclusive right to exploit all trade with China, the East Indies, and the South Sea islands, Spanish claims notwithstanding. Fifty thousand more shares were issued and snatched up before they could hit the counter. Still nobody went to Louisiana, not even for a look. Nothing was *done*, except on paper. The furore that swept the land never was in America, never on the banks of the Father of Waters, but only, alas, in the cloud-cuckoo land of French high finance.

The year after *that*, 1720, the bubble burst. The bottom fell out of the market. Law fled. There was a spate of suicides.

The Mississippi Scheme should have served as a monument to folly, a warning to all future generations of the instability of dreams. It did not. The men of America were on the make; money was everything to them; and when they were given a whole new land to play with, it was natural that they should lose their heads and often their savings as well. There was no stock exchange in the country, and there were no casinos. Political stakes were not high, nor was social life. But there was unlimited land out there beyond the mountains, and even the men who did not go clumping through the passes or paddling down the tricky streams on a westward track never lost sight of this fact. Speculation was rife in all the eastern states, not least in New England, where sea commerce might have been thought to take care of all spare capital and the moth-flame lure of risk. Soldiers of the dissolved Continental Army, and especially their officers, had largely been paid off with western acreage, land most of them never expected to see, and they sold this to dealers, who sold it to other dealers, who sold it to yet others, always at a higher price. They dealt in large tracts, these gamblers. A thousand acres, to one of them, was a mere backyard, a cabbage patch. They were not unaware of the fact that work would be needed to clear those golden fields, to raise those golden crops; but meanwhile there was money to be made just with maps and deeds and binders, and they meant to make it.[17]

Land speculation was respectable. George Washington, Benjamin Franklin, Patrick Henry, indulged in it. Washington, eager for point-at-able results, for something more than marks on papers, at one time thought of settling his own vast western lands with peasants imported from the Palatinate; but he gave up this plan, perhaps because it would have cost too much.

If in the East some speculators tended to be, comparatively, conservative, in the West *anything* went. It was before the time of the "smart" American businessman, but only a little before: on the sunset side of the Alleghenies the type was emergent.

One of the very last acts of the Continental Congress, before it gave way in 1789 to a government under the new constitution, resolved "that the free navigation of the River Mississippi is a clear and essential right of the United States, and that the same ought to be considered and supported as such." These were words. The incomers were much too busy on their own side of the mountains, at first, to give them firmness. William Blount came from North Carolina, a member of an old and respected family, but his business interests were largely in Tennessee, which then was a part of North Carolina, where he shuffled the deeds to thousand-acre tracts as casually as though they were cards at a card table. His chief interest was in a place called Muscle Shoals, near the great bend of the Tennessee.[18] With other backers, he hoped to connect this by means of a canal with the Tombigbee River, and so with the Gulf of Mexico. There was nothing small about the scheme, which would have circumvented the troublesome Mississippi, opening to the sea the products of a vast spread of land. That this was all Indian land, belonging in perpetuity to the Chickasaw and the Creeks, did not for an instant trouble William Blount and his associates. Unfortunately Spain, owning West Florida, controlled the mouth of the Tombigbee, as she controlled the mouths of all the other rivers that emptied into the Gulf. The Muscle Shoals partners, perhaps with good reason, perhaps instinctively, distrusted Spain. The government of the United States at the time was seated at Philadelphia, but it was a shaky organization at best and appeared to be irretrievably in the hands of men who believed in keeping faith with the redskins. Blount was a United States senator, but he found that he could do nothing; so he turned, naturally enough, to Great Britain. A drive down from Canada soon would scatter the dons, and Blount and his friends were prepared to help in the financing of such an expedition. He wrote to this effect to friends in England, asking them to see what they could do, but one of his letters went astray and fell into the hands of somebody who turned it over to President Adams, who without comment submitted it to Congress.

The resultant hullabaloo was deafening. Blount was called a traitor, and there were those who, like Abigail Adams, thought that he should be *"hanged."* George Washington himself was shocked. The Senate expelled Blount, and because of this—because the man no longer was a senator—impeachment proceedings were ruled out of that body on January 11, 1799, by a vote of 14 to 11, for lack of jurisdiction. It would have been the first impeachment trial in United States history.

Blount, bewildered, was in North Carolina at the time, and wisely he decided not to go back to Philadelphia. He went instead to Tennessee, where folks could not see anything wrong with what he had done: after all, it was business, wasn't it? The Muscle Shoals project fell through, but when Tennessee became a state William Blount was elected its governor.[19]

There were many such crashes, many calls for outside help, though there was none that attracted as much attention as did the Blount Conspiracy. Never, however, was there another real estate scandal so dirty, and so widespread in its malific effects, as the Yazoo case.

The Yazoo is a no-account but rather pretty little river that empties into the Mississippi a bit above Vicksburg. The name by some is considered catchy. A young songwriter in Pittsburgh, years after our time here, a man named Stephen Foster, was to take it for the first line of a tune he had just written, a tune ending with its own title, "The Old Folks at Home." The song must be about the South, for southern songs were what were selling, and Foster, though talented, was no innovator. He proposed to start it, then: " 'Way Down upon the Yazoo River." He had never been there himself—he had never been south of Cincinnati—but he liked the sound of the word. A friend, who didn't like that sound, dissuaded him, and just before publication Foster changed it to "the Swanee River," a stream, his atlas told him, that rose in Georgia and flowed through Florida to the Gulf, thus being indisputably southern. His atlas told him wrong: perhaps it was a misprint. The word was and still is *Suwanee*, spelled and pronounced in three syllables; but Foster thought that it was Swanee, two syllables, which was what he wanted, so he took it, immortalizing it; for this was by far his greatest success, bringing him almost $15,000.

It was Richard Henry Lee of Virginia who, three weeks before the adoption of the Declaration of Independence, had introduced into the Second Continental Congress the ambitiously entitled Articles of Confederation and Perpetual Union, and a committee to which they had been referred reported favorably on them July 12, after which Congress debated them off and on until the fall of 1777, when it adopted them and passed them on to the states for ratification. However, they did not go into effect until March of 1781. The reason for this delay, though the need for some such organization had long been patent, was the reluctance of the smaller states, and especially Maryland, to ratify the Articles as long as the larger states insisted upon the retention of their lands west of the mountains.

The situation there was verily a mess. Connecticut was sending troops into the Wyoming Valley of Pennsylvania, which she claimed; New York and New Hampshire were squabbling and sometimes fighting physically over Vermont, not yet a state; Pennsylvania and Virginia were arguing about their western boundaries, the principal stake being Fort Pitt, soon to become Pittsburgh; North Carolina and Virginia, the biggest transmontane claimants of all, simply could not agree on which owned what; and so it went. The smaller eastern states that did not have access to the West—New Jersey, Delaware, Maryland—insisted that all these claims be turned over to the federal government; and Maryland held out until they *were*.

The Articles of Confederation have not fared well with historians,[20] nor did they last long in fact, being replaced by the Constitution on November 21, 1788. But they were a step in the right direction, and they at least started to solve the western land problem by dumping it into the lap of Congress, which made a fairly valiant effort to protect the rights of the Indians against the machinations of land-ravenous speculators.

Georgia, always a little apart, did not take this agreement seriously. Georgia had claimed that by her original charter her territory extended clear to the Mississippi River, and even after the adoption of the Articles of Confederation and Perpetual Union, as well as after the later adoption of the Constitution of the United States, she went right on believing that this vast expanse of live oak and beech, magnolia, bay, japonica, Cape jasmine, long- and short-leaved pine, white oak, red oak, pecan, hickory, poplar, sassafras, and swampland—a region roamed only by the red men, though a smattering of it, near Natchez, did contain a few white tobacco and indigo planters—was hers to do with as she wished.

In the fall of 1787 the state blithely set up Bourbon County in the Natchez district, trying to act, afterward, as though nothing had happened. Administratively, it was proved, this simply couldn't be done. The wilderness between the new seat of government and the sponsoring state swarmed with Creeks, whose principal chief, Alexander McGillivray, violently objected, and so did the Spaniards to the south in New Orleans and to the north in the recently established fort at Chickasaw Bluffs, which today is Memphis. Bourbon County quietly ceased to exist.

A few years later, the Georgia legislature, working under the Constitution now, sold at bargain prices the triangle pointed by Chickasaw Bluffs, Muscle Shoals, and Natchez, a matter of almost 35,000,000 rich acres, to three just-organized land companies. These companies couldn't pay, or else would not meet the terms in the time allowed, and the deal fell through.

All unabashed, the legislature did the same thing again, in 1795, when it passed the infamous Yazoo Act. There were four tossed-together companies this time, and they got the land for an average of 1½¢ an acre. All four began to sell shares like mad, and prices soared, the Yankees of New England—who until this time had not taken any part in the western land scramble—being among the loudest bidders.

Then some spoilsport back home learned—and published the fact—that every member of the legislature, with a single exception, owned stock in one or the other of the favored companies. It was stock that he had only recently, and mysteriously, obtained.

(The name of the single exception, who should be esteemed a hero, has not survived; and neither has his reason for not getting in on the gravy. Perhaps he was too drunk to sign a receipt? Or, he *could* have been honest.)

Of course there was a squawk, and the following year the new legislature annulled the Yazoo Act. This was done publicly, and with a flourish. The official copy of the law was destroyed "by the fury of the sun"—that is, by means of a burning lens—in the presence of the governor, the lieutenant governor, and many other important persons.

Meanwhile, all over the nation, shares of the four companies had been sold and resold, and resold yet again. They were everywhere. Their owners appealed to Congress. *Could* a state undo such an act, an act upon which so much money rode?

There were many lawsuits, and the hard feeling went on for years. Against the bitterest sort of opposition Congress at last appropriated $4,282,151.12½ to be used in full payment of all claims, the sum having been arrived at by some calculator who remains anonymous; and the Supreme Court, 16 March 1810, in *Fletcher* v. *Peck*, confirmed this. A group of Boston banks got most of the money.

Thus the matter was concluded, on paper. There were to be many echoes, most of them discordant, though one smacked of the ludicrous.

Henry Clay was sometimes called Harry of the West, and he liked that. A good poker player, a man who could hold his liquor, he was notably amiable. History was to dub him the Great Compromiser, for he liked to patch things up between legislators seemingly at hopeless odds with one another. He did as much as any man for the settlement of the Yazoo claims, an activity for which John Randolph of Roanoke, a delegate to Congress from Virginia, and a master of vituperation, would never forgive him. Randolph was vain to the verge of madness, perhaps beyond. He was unfailingly acerbic. It was said of him that he had been born sneering, and that he carried lemon juice in his mouth instead of spit.

The Supreme Court had settled the matter; but John Randolph ran on, and on. One day from the floor of the House he called upon the parents of Henry Clay (who were dead) to weep because they had brought into the world a creature "so brilliant, yet so corrupt, which, like a rotten mackerel by moonlight, shines and stinks." This was too much even for Harry of the West, and he challenged.

When challenged on a previous occasion, "I cannot descend to your level," Randolph had coldly replied. That time it had been General James Wilkinson, a man, admittedly, so touchy about his honor that it was apparent even to those who didn't know him that he had none. But you could not talk like that to Henry Clay. The man who would rather be right than President, just at that time happened to be secretary of state, while his opponent was chairman of the House ways and means committee.

Randolph did however insist upon one unusual provision in the cartel. It was at that time *de rigueur* for governmental duelists to repair to a location in Bladensburg, Maryland, a place sometimes called the Vale of Chance. It might have been designed for their purposes. It was small and secluded. It was itself flat, but there were hills on three sides, and on the fourth was the Washington-Baltimore highway—only about fifty yards away, but well screened by trees and underbrush. The spot was about five miles from the center of Washington, but only about half a mile outside the District of Columbia. Regarding this spot Randolph of Roanoke demurred. Histrionic always, with a fervency not to be tut-tutted he vowed that if he was going to fall in the field he must fall on the soil of his beloved Virginia; and after a while the others agreed to cross the Potomac to a selected spot just above the bridge at Little Falls. They also agreed that the meeting should take place in the afternoon instead of at dawn, as was the custom. Randolph did not like to get up early.

It was a very high-toned affair. But there was still another variance from the routine of the duello.

A second had certain precautions he must take if he was to do right by his principal. Should he win the toss he must take long strides when pacing the distance, unless his friend was a poor shot, in which case the shorter the better. The duelist must be warned not to wear woolen underwear, no matter how chill the morning. It could infect a wound. He must be reminded at the last minute to urinate, for a hit in the lower abdomen, always a possibility, especially when down-pointed pistols were to be raised for firing—as was the case in the Clay-Randolph contest—could smash a bladder that had been full and cause painful complications. Most earnestly of all, the second must adjure his principal not to wear anything white. White could catch the eye and guide it. A jabot, a white cravat, the ends of a handkerchief protruding from a breast pocket, even a glimpse of shirt between breeches and waistcoat not properly tugged down, were taboo.

Once again Randolph of Roanoke proved a nonconform-
ist. He wore *only* white. Over his trousers, over his coat—and
it reached almost to his feet—he wore a loose dressing robe.
It looked like a nightgown, or, as they would have said then,
a night rail. It was ridiculous. And it was all white.

The pistols were loaded with plenty of powder and
ounce-and-a-half balls. The field was measured, and the principals placed, the guns being put into their hands muzzle
down. The signal was called.

Randolph fired into the ground, whether purposely or
from nervousness was not clear. Nobody knew what happened to Clay's bullet. Somebody started to suggest that this
should end the affair, but Clay, as was his right, insisted upon
another shot.

The guns were reloaded and recocked and placed again
in the principals' hands. The signal was called for the second
time.

Randolph fired into the earth. Clay fired fairly straight.
His ball pierced that outlandish dressing robe, though it did
not even graze the man inside. Whereupon John Randolph
threw down his weapon and stalked to Henry Clay with extended hand; and Clay threw down *his* weapon, and shook
the hand. Everybody bowed to everybody else, and they all
went off to get a drink.

6

Speak with Forked Tongue

WHEN MEN CROSSED THE ALLEGHENIES they emerged into a new and different America. Some of the problems were the same as those they had faced in the East, but others were different, and even those that could be put into the same general class assumed strangely different forms, calling for different treatment.

The Indians, excepting always the Iroquois of New York, never gave the seacoast colonists much trouble. Their ferocity was romanticized by their conquerors. But the Indians were number one on the overmountain men's complaint list.

The Indians frightened at first. They *looked* formidable. But in the case of the Indians the Pilgrims knew, for instance, it was to prove that they had been so stricken by a recent disease—probably smallpox—as to be scarcely able to stand, much less to fight effectively; and a little brutal pushing around, something the newcomers were quite capable of, soon cowed them. It was so, too, in Virginia. It was so all up and down the coast.

The exception was important. The semi-fabulous hero Hiawatha, who was a Mohawk of the Turtle clan,[21] had performed a miracle when he got the Senecas, the Oneidas, and the Onondagas to go along with the Mohawks and the Cayugas, forming the powerful Five Nations. Ordinarily American Indians—it was their most marked weakness—did not work together or consent to fight together against the white man. The members of the Five Nations, later to be joined by the Tuscaroras, who trekked up from North Carolina for the occasion, making it the Six Nations, were known collectively as the Iroquois. They were a people to be reckoned with, and indeed they *were* reckoned with—both the English and the French in their long bitter wars for control of the North American continent dangled gifts and sweet promises before them.

The Iroquois confederacy had endured for a long time, but in the era of the American Revolution it was beginning to come apart. There were fields around most of the Indian villages, places for the raising of cabbages and beans, and the community torture rack, which once had been common, seldom was seen. The bow and the quiverful of arrows had given way to the musket—usually an old and unreliable one— and the Indian had become dependent upon the white man for his powder and ball. Also, strong drink was taking its toll. The Iroquois were great in memory, but not what they once had been. They seldom conferred, now. They were not yet tame, but they were taming.

There was more room in the West. Also, there were more Indians, who by this time knew what to expect and were not likely to take white promises seriously.

Relations with the white man never were good. The Indian felt that he was being pushed out of his hunting grounds, as indeed he was. That there was goodwill toward him among the senators and congressmen in faraway Philadelphia or New York or, a little later, Washington, was something he found it hard to take on faith when he saw the more local, more immediate members of that race, the great shovers. He rebelled only from time to time, being, as always, poorly led, and not organized for war. There had been Pontiac, a genius, who kept the Ottawa, the Ojibwa, and the Potawatomi together for a little while; but after Pontiac got himself killed in a drunken brawl the league broke up and the various tribes began to fight one another again as though the white man had never appeared. Nor could another Pontiac be expected. The redskin simply could not administrate; he was not a responsible community member.

The West broke naturally into two portions, the north and the south, divided, exactly, by the Ohio River. Pontiac and his friends had come from the north, from the region that the federal government of the new republic was to call the Northwest Territory.

While the English held military control over this country, before, during, and for many years after the Revolution—for a long time they refused to evacuate the forts, contending that the Americans were not living up to *their* treaty obligations—the Indians were reasonably quiet. They did not trust the Englishmen, who didn't trust them, but the men in the red coats obviously were not greedy for land and sought only to buy the Indian's furs, paying well for these, without taking away his means of getting more. When John Buckskin appeared on the scene the atmosphere changed. It became common for Buckskin and his associates to say that you could never trust an Indian. Treaties would be solemnly made, solemnly sealed, and almost immediately violated. The chiefs meant well. Such sachems as Tahgahjute (known among the white men as Logan) and Mkahday-wah-mayquah (more familiarly, Blackfish) signed treaties in the honest belief that they would help to avert bloodshed; but the young bucks of the tribe did not see it that way, for to them every time a treaty was signed it meant that more land was shut off, and they were made angry by this, so that they went out and killed and scalped a few white men—or women. To this the nearby whites responded by descending unexpectedly upon the nearest huddle of wigwams and bashing in the heads of three or four men, women, or children. It didn't make any difference *which* men, women, or children these were, or what tribe they belonged to, or who was their chief. It was enough that their skins were red. Treaties? Bah!

Each time the Indians behaved this way it was known as an outrage; each time the white men did so it was called a defensive action.

The Northwest Territory eventually was to become the states of Ohio, Indiana, Illinois, Michigan, and Wisconsin. Thomas Jefferson, when he was secretary of state, had suggested another future for it. A dogged pacifist, he believed that the Indian troubles would somehow right themselves, and that all would be well if the territory was divided into ten equal-sized, roughly square states, to be called, inexorably: Polypotamia, Saratoga, Assenisippia, Sylvania, Washington, Illinois, Michigania, Pelisipia, Metropotamia, and Cherronesus. Nothing was done about this suggestion.

At the very outset of the Revolution it was timorously proposed to the newly appointed commander-in-chief of the Continental Army that the war about to begin should be conducted with what today we would call guerrilla tactics—that is, hit-and-run raids, swamp-dodging, sniping, supply-train cutting, swift sallies, swifter retreats. It would take many years to develop a European-type army, a stand-up army, Washington was reminded. Such an army—and the British had the best in the world then—was geared to operate on an open, laid-out battlefield. Its members knew nothing about protecting themselves from sudden assault. They would be lost if attacked Indian-fashion. The American, on the other hand, always liked to be *behind* something. He did not fire on signal, on command, in precalculated volleys, but singly, individually, and after having picked his own target. The British navy could readily plug every American port through which supplies might be received, making the home team dependent upon the hinterland. Why, then, shouldn't that team *operate* in the hinterland, leaping out from time to time, striking, leaping back? In other words, why shouldn't we fight them with what we had instead of trying to fight them with what *they* had?

George Washington of course waved this proposal away, making no memorable comment as he did so, though undoubtedly he was shocked and perhaps disgusted. His was the conventional eighteenth-century military mind, which called for upright, properly placed soldiers, every button in place, every bayonet. War was something that was conducted according to certain rules by gentlemen, and gentlemen don't crouch behind trees. War was a formalized game, like chess, in which each move called for a prearranged countermove. Washington probably never gave a second thought to the suggestion that he fight as the aborigines did. He was too well brought up for that.

Even in the wilderness the white Americans tended to battle in stand-up fashion, to the delight of their foes. From a military point of view they were not an admirable lot. The regulars were poorly paid, poorly equipped; they were mostly foreigners, and quick to desert. The militia, upon which most of the reliance was placed, was even worse. Militiamen were here today and gone tomorrow. They were always worried about their crops back home. As soon as they had succeeded in felling a few redskins they would break up and take their separate paths back to their separate cabins—and as like as not be ambushed on the way, with bloody results. In virtually all battles in the Northwest, whether large or small—though they were all small by conventional standards—the Indians, seldom seen, got the best of it. The Indian was not notably wily, but he was an instinctual fighter, and he kept out of sight. Not until the memorable field of Fallen Timbers did the Indians, a heterogeneous lot, unamenable, as always, to central command, unexpectedly decide to come into the open and slug it out, thus permitting the white men, under "Mad Anthony" Wayne, to beat the devil out of them. Afterward the whites, still astounded, made a vicious if scattered chase, killing right and left, with a whoop.[22]

After Fallen Timbers the Hurons, Miamis (Wyandots), Chippewa, Sacs, Delaware, Potawatomis, and Ottawa never again tried to form a league of any sort. They sued for peace, separately. Even the Shawnee sued, headdresses in hand. Each tribe gave up even more land; and they were never to be any real trouble again.

In the *South*west Territory it was not the same. There the distances were greater, the rivers wider, the air hotter, the swamps darker and more treacherous. The Indians of the Southwest Territory were more nearly "civilized" than those anywhere else in America north of Mexico. They would take their share of scalps, and they liked to slow-burn a prisoner to death now and then, but long-drawn-out torture was not a passion with them, as it had been with the Iroquois and as it was to be with tribes farther west. Whole villages would not turn out to spend all night watching and listening to some poor rack-trussed wretch being picked to pieces, his eyes plucked out, his fingernails one by one, his flesh in tiny red chunks. The enjoyment of hideous pain, though they were not unacquainted with it, was not a way of life with the Chickasaw, the Cherokee, the Choctaw, the Creeks. Moreover, they all spoke the same tongue, Muskogean, so that they could understand one another and, if they cared to, co-operate, even though they might live far apart.

The Chickasaw were the smallest tribe, and the friendliest to Americans, though they hated the French. The Cherokee were the most intelligent. The Choctaw, it was said, could put five thousand warriors into the field, but they were a lazy lot and seldom came out of their murky forests. The Creeks were at once the most numerous and most warlike, the nearest, at the same time, to the Americans and to the Spaniards.

Much has been made of the so-called Creek Confederacy, and a student might come to believe that one whistle would summon all the indigenes of the Southwest Territory, armed, on tiptoe, and waiting only for the nod of a pre-selected master to send them screaming at their foe. This was not the case. The Chickasaw, the Creeks, the Choctaw, and the Cherokee did not waste themselves in civil strife, but they were a proud, individualistic people, and they obeyed many chiefs—when they consented to obey any at all.

The Creeks, it was reckoned, could put 6,000 warriors into the field, the Cherokees 2,000, Chickasaw 500, Choctaw 5,000—a total of 13,500, or more than *four times* the size of the entire strewn-out United States Army in the 1790s. But they never *were* all in the field at the same time, and it did not seem likely that they ever would be.

The Chickamaugas, for example, were a small independent branch of the Cherokee, and a notably scrappy group too, a people for whom the rest of the tribe often apologized. The Creeks themselves had been split into the Upper Creeks, who were to harass the first new-state movements of Franklin, Wantaugh, and Holston, and the Lower Creeks, who, on the other hand, directly faced the Georgians just south of the mountains. There was also a large breakaway tribal segment who called themselves the Seminoles, but these had gone deep into East Florida, and, though they spoke the same language, from a military point of view they might as well have been living on the moon.

There had once been a Natchez tribe, inhabiting the Yazoo lands long before the coming of the real estate agents. The Natchez (pronounced Nat-*chay*) spoke a Muskogean dialect. They flattened the heads of their babies, and practiced a curious and very rigid caste system. There might have been four thousand of them at one time; but in 1729 they offended the French, who thereupon wiped them out. A few of the females escaped to the Chickasaw and the Cherokee, where they denied their origin, changing their names—for the French were thorough about seeking them out and slaughtering them—while a few hundred of the men, taken captive, were shipped as slaves to the West Indies, where undoubtedly they died an early death, for the Indians never did make good slaves.

The Natchez shared the fate of many another small tribe both east and west of the mountains—the Timucua, the Calusa, and the Apalachee Indians, for instance, and the Powhatans and the Nanticokes. These simply disappeared, for the white man had found them inconvenient. Others, of course, like the Patuxents of New England and the Mandans of the Dakota country, were wiped out by disease.

Northwest and Southwest the Indians professed to scorn the white man and his ways, yet they were becoming increasingly dependent upon him. They dabbled in agriculture, especially the best organized of them—the Iroquois and the Lower Creeks—but this remained a chore for the squaws. However, north and south alike, squaws and warriors, they were living what was for them a soft life. Glass beads and mirrors might be all right for festive occasions, but the Indian wanted to be sure that he did not have to sign another treaty in order to get a steady supply of firewater. He and his kind could not dream, now, of living without blankets, and these blankets they bought from the white man, who got them from England, where they were woven. Even the braves' tomahawks no longer were chipped-stone striking instruments, but were, rather, steel-headed hatchets manufactured in large quantities in the factories of the East. Why, their very *war paint* came from abroad, most of it from Germany.

These things were not free. They must be paid for with the only currency the red man knew—furs. An occasional head of cabbage was all very well, but the Indian had to hunt to live, and in order to hunt he had to have land. Pelts as currency were not a new notion in those parts. The states that sprang up so exuberantly in the early days of the frontier not infrequently had nothing but the hides of animals for their cash. The employees of the Wantaugh government, which lasted for five years, were paid with pelts. So were those of Franklin, which lasted three. The governor of Franklin got one thousand deerskins a year, or was supposed to get them; his secretary, five hundred coonskins; a justice of the peace was paid four muskrat pelts for signing a warrant, and the constable who served same was paid a mink skin. But this was, for them, a temporary arrangement. It was all that the Indians had, or could look forward to.

7

An Improbable Hero

THERE WERE VARIOUS KINDS of white men in the West.
The English on the whole treated the Indians well,
though, according to the first buckskin invaders, who called
them "hair buyers," they went too far when they paid a
bounty for fresh scalps. When individual Englishmen who
had trading business with Indians traveled among them, they
took on redskinned "wives" for the trip, as seemed to be expected; but they did not *marry* these women.

The French always had made it a part of their policy to
mix with the red men, learning their languages, practicing
their ways, even dancing their dances, but there never had
been many Frenchmen in America at best, and they were
widely scattered. They were almost unknown in the Southwest Territory. James Girty, a nephew of the notorious rene-
gade Simon Girty, sometimes was seen in those parts, and
James Colbert sired a famous line of Chickasaw chiefs. Colbert, French to the core, was better known, however, for his
stable of slaves. The Southwest Indians, who never had seen
a Negro who was *not* a slave, treated runaways from bondage
in exactly that manner, whether they came from the Spanish

in Florida and Louisiana, or around the lower part of the mountains from the planters of Georgia and the Carolinas. To the Muskogean-speaking redskins they were acceptable, but they were made to work like squaws, were not allowed to marry, and were given, in fact, no privileges. James Colbert at one time was said to have had one hundred Negro slaves.

The Spaniard was no fool, though he sometimes seemed to be. His rigidity, his perfervid religiosity, his insistence upon the trivialities of pomp, and his melancholy did not prevent him from understanding, realistically, his world position. He was outmoded and he knew it. The imperial system to which he clung was a system doomed to death, indeed halfway there. The gilt of Spanish America had begun to flake and to fall off, and soon the whole structure would collapse.

Once Spain had fought for her splendid possessions; but the days of the conquistadores were gone, and Louisiana had simply been handed to Spain because Spain happened to be there, a token, a pledge, a thing to be handed back as soon as France was in a position again to manage it. Spain's representatives in New Orleans knew this. As far as the Escorial was concerned, they knew that Louisiana was no more than a bit of outside protection for Mexico. Spain was almost insanely jealous of Mexico, her richest and most productive possession, and she watched cagily while the greedy Yanks worked their way south. For Louisiana itself she had no plans. Parisians of John Law's day had believed that the territory was crammed with precious metals, but the Spaniards never believed that, and they never did try to settle Louisiana, to colonize the place. They maintained a few officials and soldiers in a few fortified places, and that was all. New Orleans remained preponderantly French. It had only a nuisance value for the Spaniards.

The pushers from the North, however, were not easily held off. It was obvious that, if they ever got angry enough, no matter what their faraway government might say they

could take New Orleans overnight, for it was a flat city with
no fortifications at all and merely a nominal garrison. The
Spaniards themselves were not strong enough to parry such
a stroke, nor could they depend upon Great Britain, with
which they were at war more often than not, or France,
which itself was hungrily eyeing a Louisiana it had once
owned. So the Spaniards turned to the Indians, and specifically and especially to the Indians of the old Southwest—the
Choctaw, Chickasaw, Creeks, and Cherokee. They promised
to help them keep their lands, even though those lands now
belonged to the new republic of the United States. They fur-
nished them with gunpowder and ball, sometimes with firewater too. They coddled them.

Unexpectedly, the most successful mixers with those
Southwestern Indians were the Scots.

William MacIntosh was such a one. He adopted the Indian ways and learned the Indian speech with as much
aplomb as any *coureur de bois;* he married a Creek maiden,
and his sons were all chiefs. There were, too, Alexander
Fraser and Alexander Cameron; and in truth the shout of
"Sandy!" must have sounded many times through many an
aborigine village in those days.

John Chisholm came across the sea as a captain in the
British army, and when the Revolution was over he stayed
on, settling as an Indian trader and justice of the peace in
Knoxville, Tennessee. He never did actually join a tribe, but
he lived with the Indians for long stretches, and could talk
with them. He was William Blount's personal Indian agent.

Panton & Leslie, a British outfit, was easily the most in-
fluential and the most successful fur-trading firm in that part
of the world, and indeed almost had a monopoly on the
business. Both William Panton and Robert Leslie were Scot-
tish, and they lived in America, much of the time out in the
wilderness among their customers. All their working assist-
ants, too—like John Forbes, like Kenneth Ferguson—were
Scots.

A little after our period here, when the federal government began to build military roads through the Creek and Cherokee country, it became the custom to rent the ferrying privileges to half-breeds, some of whom made a very good thing of this. There were many ferries in that stream-striped world, and travelers never failed to mention the fact that the operators, when they could be induced to talk at all—for they were a surly lot—spoke with a decided burr.

The greatest by far of Caledonia's contributions to the red race was Alexander McGillivray, sometimes called "the King of the Creeks," sometimes "the Talleyrand of Alabama."

Here was a most improbable hero. The American red man admired physical prowess to the exclusion of almost every other virtue, much as did Europeans in the days when knighthood was more or less in flower. Regard for it, and discussion of it, were to the Indian an institution. Except for the sainted Tammany, a Delaware sachem, their outstanding chiefs were noted rather for their savagery than for their sagacity. Pontiac, Tecumseh, Crazy Horse, Sitting Bull, and Geronimo might have been wise men, for all we know now, but it was not wisdom that gave them their influence over their fellow Indians; it was rather their willingness to take scalps, to venture close to the enemy. By way of contrast, Alexander McGillivray, a tall erect man with large, dark, deep-set eyes under beetling brows, suffered all his life from ill health. He drank too much too often. He hated any form of fighting, and indeed the sight of blood made him sick. He lived quietly, but well, on a plantation on the Coosa River, not far from the present city of Montgomery, and at one time he was said to own as many as sixty Negro slaves. He always protested that he was not *the* chief of the Creeks, as so many white men appear to think, but only *a* chief. They did not believe this. A man so regal in manner must be a king, they thought. They would come to him from the outside world, some of them exceedingly distinguished men, commissioners, generals, senators, and hold high their outfacing palms, and cry "How!" and get off some quaint sayings in what they thought was pidgin. They would be answered in impeccable English, which was disconcerting.

His father had been Lachlan McGillivray, who came from Scotland before the Revolution and made a fortune dealing with the Creeks—and living with them. He made most of that money speculating in lands in Georgia proper, not in the Creek country. His estate there alone was said to be worth $100,000. He married a celebrated half-breed beauty, Sehoy Marchard, whose father had been French, and their son, Alexander, therefore, was one half Scottish, one quarter Creek, and one quarter French, a stimulating combination.

Lachlan, come the Revolution, was staunchly loyal, as were most Scots in America, though many of them had fought against the House of Hanover and for the House of Stuart in the course of Prince Charlie's doings of 1745–1746 and, indeed, were in America for that very reason. Because of this loyalty to England Lachlan McGillivray saw his Georgia property confiscated. Just before he skipped back to Scotland, in order to save his own skin, McGillivray Senior bequeathed this claim to his son among the Indians. It impressed white visitors by its very existence, but it had nothing to do with the young McGillivray's high standing among the Creeks, who never believed that he could collect on it anyway (and he never did), for in their experience almost any white man would sooner give up his life than give up his land.

Alexander's tribal name—his, as it were, *baptismal* name —was Hoboi-Hili-Miko, which means Good Child King, suggesting that his mother had high hopes for his future, a condition common to many mothers. She was a Wind; and this made all the difference. Among the Creeks matriarchy prevailed as far as all inheritance was concerned, and so Alexander too was a member of the Wind clan, which almost automatically made him a chief or, at least, eligible to a chiefship.

As was natural, Alexander McGillivray hated the Americans. Anyway, he saw the Spaniards as the best friends of his fellow tribesmen, and he played ball with them. Since there were no Spanish fur dealers, he took up with his fellow Scots of that business, Panton & Leslie. He was a close friend of William Panton, and largely responsible for that firm's near-monopoly.

Even when he learned that both the governor of Louisiana and the intendant were financially interested in another trading firm, stationed in New Orleans, Alexander McGillivray stuck to Panton & Leslie.

One of the outmoded, almost medieval anfractuosities of Spanish imperial law provided that a province should have two on-the-spot rulers, each of equal strength though in different fields. The governor was known as "the Sword"; the intendant, a sort of high treasurer, as "the Purse." When these two got along well together everything was all right. When they didn't, it wasn't.

Don Estevan Miró, the successor to the dashing Gálvez as governor of Louisiana, and Don Martin Navarro, the intendant at that time, in fact did not get along together. They did, however, agree that the fur-trading monopoly—the Spaniards themselves simply did not have the men to conduct it, so the best they could hope for was to control it—should go to the English firm of Mather & Strother. Deep in the wilderness the inscrutable Alexander McGillivray demurred. He stuck to his friends Panton & Leslie, which must have taken courage. And his will prevailed.

When the state of Georgia exuberantly tried to assert its so-called rights to all the territory west of the mountains as far as the Mississippi itself, the effort taking the form of the establishment of the county of Bourbon in Yazoo territory, the hidden McGillivray spoke again, and again his voice was the final one. This time he behaved in an uncharacteristic fashion. He sent an independent war party to the country near the mouth of the Yazoo, and these warriors, in the course of an apparently haphazard attack upon Georgian property, saw to it that the delegate from Georgia, one Davenport, upon whose presence the whole venture depended, got "accidentally" killed. The Georgians could take a hint. They were more than a thousand miles from their beloved Bourbon County, and Alexander McGillivray, who controlled those miles, had stated his position. The Georgians, teetering on the edge of a war they knew they could not afford, withdrew. There were those, even among the happy Spaniards, who muttered that maybe Big Chief McGillivray was getting too big for his loincloth; and certainly he never moved a finger to deny the charge that he had ordered Davenport's murder; but his position remained strong.

There came into the Creek country at this time a younger man who quickly learned the language and assumed for himself a place of importance among the Indians, though he had none of their blood. William Augustus Bowles was an eccentric. He wore rows of beads around his neck, and he went about in his bare feet; but he knew his fur prices. He had been a musician, a portrait painter, an actor. He was now the representative of Miller, Bonnamy & Co., of Nassau, New Providence Island, the West Indies, a company headed by Lord Dunmore, still another Scot, the last royal governor of Virginia and presently governor of the Bahamas. Bowles, clanking his trinkets, brought gifts to Alexander McGillivray, an earnest of his intention to stay in the wilderness. McGillivray accepted them without comment, and, being an Indian, he did not stoop to say "Thank you." He was taking gifts from the Spaniards all this while, and soon he was about to take them too from the Americans. He was criticized for this, but he couldn't see why. Indians always accepted gifts from anyone; and they *never* said "Thank you." It was the custom.

With the political pull and all the money of Miller, Bonnamy behind him, William Augustus Bowles might have proved a dangerous opponent of Alexander McGillivray. But he did not last long, out there in the wilderness. The Spaniards lured him to New Orleans with honeyed words, and clapped him into jail, and sent him to Spain, where, after some sort of secret trial—the whole affair was hushed up as much as possible—he was dispatched clear around the world to the Philippine Islands for safekeeping. McGillivray's influence no longer had any rival.

The Georgians kept clamoring for war, though they wanted the federal government to fight it for them. That government, so new, located temporarily in New York, more or less agreed; and the first secretary of war, Henry Knox,[23] after conferring with Anthony Wayne, drew up plans. It would have been the first United States war as an independent nation.

The President, George Washington, passed on the plans, but he persuaded Knox to make one more try for peace by appointing a commission to go into the Creek country and invite Alexander McGillivray to come to the capital and talk it over. Knox, though fat, ordinarily was a crusty party, touchy, fussy, not at all popular with his associates; but he proved that he could be a good diplomat when he tried. The commission was a distinguished one, and the commissioners did not condescend to McGillivray when he greeted them on the banks of the Coosa. McGillivray made it clear once again that he was only *a* chief of the Creeks, not *the* chief. They nodded politely, and offered to take along as many more such leaders as he should designate. He said too that he didn't want to go by sea. He was afraid of the water. Like most Indians he was a poor sailor, and his one brief experience— from Pensacola to New Orleans at the invitation of the Spaniards—had terrified him. The commissioners promised to supply horses and wagons. And so, after a great deal of palavering, and feasting, and peace-pipe smoking, thirty Creek chieftains, McGillivray among them, started for New York. They had outriders, and it was an imposing procession. They were enthusiastically greeted at Richmond, Baltimore, Philadelphia. There was one short water hop. They took a ferry at

Elizabethtown Point, to enter New York from the bottom. They were made much of at the Battery, and were escorted in triumph to the executive mansion, where President Washington welcomed them in person, bestowing upon each a string of beads and a packet of tobacco. Then they all went to the City Tavern for a feast, the first of many. Their hosts at the tavern were the members of the newly formed Society of St. Tammany, Aaron Burr's creature, and each of the visitors was made an honorary sachem of this organization.

That was July 20, 1790. The conference lasted until August 14. Some of the chiefs slept at the Indian Queen Hotel, and others camped just outside town, a short walk away; but Alexander McGillivray was the personal guest of Secretary Knox at his home in Wall Street. He was made much of. The St. Andrew's Society elected him an honorary member. He was commissioned a brigadier general in the United States Army. More, he was appointed the United States Indian agent in the Lower Creek country, a job that paid $1,200 a year.[24] He did not sue for the return of his father's Georgia lands, for he never did seem much concerned with money.

The crowds were immense, wherever the visitors went, and when they began to get drunk they would usually oblige with a war dance, to the delight of the Gothamites. McGillivray himself, though a notorious toper, on these occasions remained sternly sober.

In the end, George Washington received them again, and (though he hated to touch anybody) shook each of them by the hand.

The conference was a success. The Creeks gave up a little land—this always happened when the two races got together—but they were confirmed in many of their minor rights; the Georgians were restrained from harassing them; and, best of all, war had been averted, had been at least *postponed*.

Moreover, this, the first such conference, was to be taken

as a model. The next year Governor William Blount of Tennessee held a meeting of the Chickasaw, Cherokee, and Choctaw chiefs at Nashville, but other tribes thereafter were treated to a tour of the national capital, soon to be at Washington, and the White House was to become their first and last visiting place. A pattern had been formed.

The position of Alexander McGillivray, deep in the wilderness, was stronger than ever.

William Augustus Bowles, complete with feathers, beads, and bare feet, reappeared in Alabama a few years later, having broken jail in the Philippines. He still had the backing of Miller, Bonnamy & Co. of Nassau. With a handful of followers he captured St. Mark's Fort between the Apalachee and Wakulla rivers, and he proclaimed himself to be the "General and Director of the Creek and Cherokee Nations." But he did not last long. The Spaniards, correctly assuming that he would not take their word for anything again, simply kidnapped him. The crime was committed in United States territory, but no official report was made, and so no complaint was filed. Bowles was taken to New Orleans, and then sent to Havana, where he was clapped into Morro Castle, never to be seen or heard from again.

This had nothing to do with Alexander McGillivray who, a little earlier, had died a natural death at the home of his old friend William Panton in Pensacola. He was a great man.

CHAPTER

8

The Man with a Million Dollars

A FONDNESS FOR SUPERLATIVES is said to be one of the outstanding American faults; yet there are still many who think that Theodore Roosevelt—Gamaliel Bradford was to say of him that "he killed elephants like mosquitoes, and mosquitoes like elephants"—when he characterized James Wilkinson as "the most despicable" soldier in our history, was going a mite too far.

Wilkinson, considering his limited abilities, made a very big splash indeed, but the wavelets soon subsided. He was praised; he was execrated. He had all the trappings of a villain, yet he also had many of the trappings of a hero. It was as a hero that he thought of himself; and so strenuously did he spout his heroics that there were some who came to believe him. To compare him with Benedict Arnold is just silly. He wasn't half the man that Arnold was. Today, of course, he is forgotten. Arnold never will be.

For better or for worse, anyway, James Wilkinson is inextricably tied up with the history of Old Man River.

He was born in Calvert County, Maryland, in 1757, of parents who were respectable if not rich. He studied medicine for a while, but at the outbreak of the Revolution he joined the Continental Army, where he soon showed a flair for headquarters intrigue. He was with Arnold before Quebec, and he did well enough. He was with Gates in the Saratoga campaign, and he did much better. His victories were all staff victories, not in the field. He was young, tall, handsome, and good company. Horatio Gates, the commanding general, the son of an English house servant and always aware of this fact, took a fancy to his dashing aide; and after the surrender of Burgoyne, a stunning victory for the Continentals, he named Wilkinson to carry the news to Congress.

The honor was important. It was a custom of the time to announce any considerable victory by means of a personal messenger, who, when he had reported to the king or the queen or the governing body, would be appropriately rewarded: besides a handsome gift he was sure of a promotion. This was always done. In consequence there was a scramble among the eligible young aides to get the assignment; and that James Wilkinson won, after Saratoga, was no surprise to anyone at Continental northern headquarters, where he had long been known as General Gates's white-haired boy.

This *official* delivery of the news was of course no more than a ceremony. Indeed Lieutenant Colonel Wilkinson took so long to get from Saratoga to Congress—for he was lavishly entertained along the way—that one disgruntled member remarked that a pair of spurs might be an appropriate gift. Nevertheless he was enthusiastically received when at last he made it, and he was jumped two notches in rank to a brigadier generalship. There was a howl from those who had been overleaped, no fewer than forty-seven active colonels protesting in round robin form; but the promotion stood.

It did not stand long. There was a scandal concerning some of Wilkinson's loose talk on his way from Saratoga, something about the unfitness of General Washington for the supreme command. It was never straightened out; it was never made clear. The new brigadier general, it seemed, couldn't hold his liquor. No other charge was made against him; he was not even threatened with a court martial; but he saw fit quietly to resign.

He was still in his twenties. He had married a Biddle of Philadelphia, member of a family that had shown a surpassing ability to raise funds. Soon he was back in the army, again with a general's rank, though there was no glitter attached to the new job. He became the clothier general, at a salary of $5,000 a year. He bought Trevose, the 450-acre estate that had been confiscated from the Tory-minded Joseph Galloway. It was north of Philadelphia, near Bristol, on the Delaware, and he paid $4,600 for it. He and Mrs. Wilkinson lived high there. They always lived high.

It should be mentioned that his career as clothier general, while undistinguished, never was touched by pitch. Such a post, the finances of the country being what they were at the time, surely offered large opportunities for graft; but Wilkinson, though his morals were not stern, and though he dearly loved the power that money gave and the bright things that it could buy, seems never to have been tempted to steal.

When the war was over he was in debt and, like so many men who were in debt, he went west. He settled near the present city of Louisville, at the Falls of the Ohio, and he opened a store and dealt in all kinds of merchandise. He dabbled, too, in land, presumably with money borrowed through the influence of his in-laws.

He was never a success as a businessman. He continued to live like a lord though he never caught up with his obligations; but he was well thought of by the neighbors, who admired his looks, his wife, his oratory. He was prominent in the movement to gain statehood for Kentucky, which felt that the East was neglecting it. (Despite Wilkinson's thunderings, statehood was held up until it could first be arranged for a northern applicant, Vermont, so that the North-South balance in the Senate would not be disturbed.) He could always be counted upon to express an opinion, often in words few others could understand. He would pompously utter ponderous polysyllabic piffle, which men liked to listen to. He fancied alliteration.

He thought big. In the year 1787 he had the biggest idea of all, and acted upon it. That was the beginning of the Spanish Conspiracy.

This sounds dark, it sounds dastardly. The word "conspiracy" was in fashion just at that time, and it was somewhat loosely used. The Blount Conspiracy and the Pontiac Conspiracy, for examples, hardly would be called that today. But —the Spanish Conspiracy? It draws a picture of conniving, muttering men huddled in unlit doorways, passing mysterious messages to one another. It suggests white-toothed sneers under raven-black mustachios; and torture chambers; and daggers held behind backs.

As a matter of fact, it was a misnomer. It should have been called the Wilkinson Conspiracy, or the Kentucky Conspiracy.[25] *They* conspired to approach the Spaniards. The Spaniards did not conspire to approach and to defile them.

The Conspiracy is Wilkinson's chief claim to fame, or infamy, though he always denied its existence. He did not have perfidy in his heart. He did, or tried to do, like those around him. He aspired to be one of the first "smart" American businessmen, a set that never was troubled by considerations of ethical behavior or fair play. To him the whole thing was just another deal; and any deal, if successful, is its own justification. The man with a million dollars is always right.

What James Wilkinson did, then, was load a couple of barges with tobacco, salt pork, lard, and beaver skins, and drop down the Mississippi with these, for the purpose of selling them in New Orleans.

It was a move that called for imagination and high courage. Thomas Amis and his pots and pans, which the Spaniards had seized before he could sell them in New Orleans, had not been forgotten. Nobody in the West knew where he stood with the gatekeepers of the Mississippi, the Spaniards at New Orleans. Upon them, upon their unpredictable whims, might hang the fate of a continent. Wilkinson meant to put them to the test. He would try them out, deliberately.

It was not pure patriotism that motivated him. He meant to make his pile. Nevertheless, what he did was a fine thing.

John Buckskin, facing an implacable wilderness, had only his ax and his hoe—and his rifle. He had no stored-up fat to fall back upon. No study had been made in advance of the possibilities of the territory to which he had just committed himself. He had to make an immediate living, from scratch, *his* scratch. Whatever he raised or caught could not be consumed with any profit by himself and his neighbors: it had to be sold. To send it over the mountains whence John Buckskin had just come would be a laborious and killingly expensive process. He could only send it down to the Gulf, for shipment to other places, and notably to the West Indies, where one-crop planters always were clamoring for cheap food with which to feed their slaves. But that meant going through New Orleans, where the Spaniards were; and nobody knew how the Spaniards would act at any given time. To be sure, they were corruptible, like all Spanish officials in America; but who could be sure that they would *stay* corrupted? Who could be sure that the scale of bribery might not be altered while his goods were on their way to market? Once in the Crescent City they must be sold somehow, at whatever price, or else just given away. They could not be reprocessed or returned.

The territory of Louisiana did not pay for itself, and there was no reason to believe that Spain expected it to do so.[26] The territory was a piece of padding, a strip of chafing gear. Its revenues did not amount to one-fifth of its fixed expenditures. It raised almost no exportable products of its own, and even if the through-trade of the Kentuckians was suddenly quadrupled this still would not begin to pay the expenses of maintaining a customs house in New Orleans. That tariff might be raised, or the trade might be prohibited at any moment, without warning.

Wilkinson went south in style, as was his custom. He was using, now, his title of General, and he carried with him an impressive wardrobe. When he neared New Orleans he let word trickle ahead that somebody very important was coming. It worked. He was received with ceremony by both the governor and the intendant, and he was made much of. He smiled graciously.

How the man did it we will never know. He had not at his command a word of either Spanish or French, and all his meetings with the high officials were secret. He was permitted to sell his goods publicly, and he got a good price for them. More, he was virtually promised a monopoly on the trade in tobacco from Kentucky. His own shipments, and any shipments he might see fit to put his stamp of approval on, would be permitted access to the free market in New Orleans. This should have made him rich, and in a very short time.

Of course he had to give up something. The Spaniards were not philanthropists. There were those who were to say that Wilkinson while in New Orleans took an oath to serve the king of Spain for the rest of his life, but he always denied this.[27] It is certain that this visit marked the beginning of a long correspondence between Wilkinson and the governor and later the governor's successors, a correspondence carried on in code, Wilkinson always being referred to as "Number Thirteen." It is certain too that the governor advanced Wilkinson $7,000 as a "loan," though he must have known that he would never get it back, and that he promised (he was about to retire) to recommend to his successor that Wilkinson be paid $2,000 a year by the Spanish government, which was done.

What is a spy? Had you called Wilkinson that to his face he would have challenged you to come out and meet

him on the field of honor. He would have been honestly out-
raged.

When, four years later, needing money again, or still,
Wilkinson got back into the United States Army—or, as he
put it, "resumed the sword"—it did not seem to have occurred
to him to suggest that this bribe be terminated. The $2,000
a year kept coming in, and Wilkinson indeed was involved
in an attempt, soon to be successful, to have it doubled.

What he undoubtedly did promise in New Orleans, and
what he was to deliver, was a running account of the dis-
unity operation in Kentucky. He did not *foment* discontent.
He did not need to. He simply kept his eye on the men—he
knew them all, most of them intimately—who might be
counted upon, when the time came, to break away from the
central government. He, Number Thirteen, reported regularly upon the separatist movement, of which he was one of
the leaders. But—he was not a spy. Oh, no.

After more than a month of gay living in New Orleans
he returned to Philadelphia by sea, pausing there for a time
in order to campaign against ratification of the constitution
that had just been submitted to the states. There is no reason
to think that this had anything to do with his secession work,
or anything to do with Spain. Wilkinson simply believed that
under a centralized Eastern government Kentucky would get
an even poorer deal.

The constitution was ratified anyway, and Wilkinson returned to Louisville by way of Pittsburgh.

He did not prosper, as he should have done. He brought
an offer of $9.50 a hundredweight for all the tobacco Ken-
tucky could provide, and the stuff until that time had been
selling for $2. This made Wilkinson extremely popular, for a
little while. But tobacco was a royal monopoly in Spain, and
soon word came from Madrid that the Kentucky product,
the Louisiana product as well, simply wasn't good enough;
and this market door was slammed in his face.

He should have cleaned up quickly in the meanwhile,

but he hadn't. The truth is, he seems to have been a poor businessman. All his life he was borrowing money, and he very seldom paid it back. His grand schemes always collapsed, leaving him with no reserve. He might have consoled himself with the knowledge that other figures in the new republic—Samuel Adams, for instance, and Patrick Henry—were also business failures; but he did not do this; doggedly he kept trying.

The pension did not always arrive on time, and Wilkinson was assiduous about making new proposals, as when in a letter of February 24, 1794, he suggested to Governor Carondelet of Louisiana that a $200,000 fund be set up with which to buy Kentuckians—only he did not use the word "buy." Early in December of that same year a messenger from New Orleans, Henry Owens, was murdered on the Ohio River by Spanish boatmen who then stole the six thousand Spanish dollars he was carrying in three kegs, money that was supposed to go, quietly, to James Wilkinson. Three of the boatmen were arrested and haled before Harry Innes, the United States District Court judge in Louisville. Innes, a crony of Wilkinson, was one of the leaders of the separatist movement —in other words, of the Spanish Conspiracy. He immediately sent the prisoners to the commanding officer at Fort Washington, which was Cincinnati, on the ground that as Spanish subjects they did not come within his jurisdiction. The commanding officer, James Wilkinson, was equally embarrassed, and he ordered the men sent to New Madrid, a Spanish military post on the west bank of the Mississippi, after which they disappeared from history, along with the six thousand dollars. A similar sum at the same time was going to Wilkinson by sea and from Philadelphia by way of Pittsburgh, thence on the Ohio to Louisville. What with one thing and another—there was never a real investigation—only $1,700 of it got there.

Wilkinson's work did not go entirely unrewarded. In June, 1796, 9,640 Spanish silver dollars were packed into a shipment of coffee and sugar at New Madrid and sent up the Ohio to Frankfort, where at the store of Montgomery Brown they were opened by Philip Nolan, Wilkinson's chief lieutenant at the time—he was later hanged on the banks of the Brazos, but it was a mistake—who, as directed, paid the courier, Thomas Power, $640. What Wilkinson did with the rest of the money is not a matter of record, but it is known that he did sell the sugar and the coffee, which had been duly consigned to him.

Only in the army did he prosper. The Wilkinsons had the first carriage in Cincinnati, and it was drawn by two horses, a splendid sight. When the general rode alone it was on a highstepping stallion, his stirrups and spurs made of gold or something that looked like gold, while there were gold leopard claws against his leopard saddle cloth. To be invited to the Wilkinsons' for dinner was a real treat, and most of the guests couldn't even *pronounce* the dishes or the wines. To be invited out for a trip up and down the river was an even greater treat. The general's barge was manned by twenty-five to thirty oarsmen or polers, besides the musicians, the cooks, the waiters. The general did tend, it is true, toward nepotism. His youngest son was with him to share the privations of the West, and two nephews and a brother-in-law: collectively these men were known as the House of Wilkinson. But he kept his chins up. His letters might be strewn with monstrosities like "to circumstantiate this asseveration," but he could remember to enjoin his correspondents to caution, for "there are spies everywhere!" To Governor Gayoso of Louisiana he wrote: "Never suffer my name to be written or spoken. The suspicion of Washington is wide awake." And he could confess to President Adams that "it is the invisibility of my enemies only which I fear, for while I dare the open assault, I dread the secret stab."

Adams did not trust him, any more than had Washington, but each President, knowing that proof of guilt would be hard to find, hoped that high rank would sober the general and perhaps cause him to abstain from sending *too much* information to the dons. It was true that he never used one word when ten could do the job, but it was true too that he had about him a very high-class air, and when General Wayne died at Presque Isle, Pennsylvania, General Wilkinson's last high-placed enemy no longer stood in his way, and he became, incredibly, by rote, the commander-in-chief of the United States Army.

President Jefferson liked him well enough, though he never really trusted him. General Wilkinson used to send him soil and mineral samples from the West. Indeed, the American Philosophical Society elected Wilkinson a member because of his interest in Indian antiquities.

But he still owed money.

In 1792 Kentucky was at last admitted to the Union, the fifteenth state; but the separation movement did not die, though it did wobble for a little while. General Wilkinson still addressed the conventions that Kentuckians always were calling; and resolutions determinedly shaking a fist at the federal government still were passed with an undismayed regularity. It gave Kentuckians a cause, something they had hitherto lacked. As Henry Adams was to put it: [28]

In the early days of colonization, every new settlement represented an idea and proclaimed a mission. Virginia was founded by a great, liberal movement aiming at the spread of English liberty and empire. The Pilgrims of Plymouth, the Puritans of Boston, the Quakers of Pennsylvania, all avowed a moral purpose, and began by making institutions that consciously reflected a moral idea. No such character belonged to the colonization of 1800. From Lake Erie to Florida, in long, unbroken line, pioneers were at work, cutting into the forests with the energy of so many beavers, and with no more express moral purpose than the beavers they drove away. The civilization they carried with them was rarely illumined by an idea; they sought room for no new truth, and aimed neither at creating, like the Puritans, a government of saints, nor, like the Quakers, one of love and peace; they left such experiments behind them, and wrestled only with the hardest problems of frontier life. No wonder that foreign observers, and even the educated, well-to-do Americans of the seacoast, could seldom see anything to admire in the ignorance and brutality of frontiersmen and should declare that virtue and wisdom no longer guided the United States!

9

He Came Like a Comet

As far back as the birth of the nation Americans had been asking one another whether Europe, in fact, was necessary, and even whether it was a good example for this new people to follow. There were isolationists before the word itself was coined, and though in the early days of the republic they were not proportionately as great as they were to become, they were great enough. Our language, our law, our literature, these came from over the sea, yes; but was it imperative to import as well from those jejune communities their prejudices, their castes, and social splittings? Most pertinent of all was the question: Can't we stay out of their ancient dirty quarrels? Must our place in the world be fenced in by their rigidities, their long-standing, warped, noxious ideas about the non-nobility of man?

The answer was inexorable. That the United States could be its own man, free of the frivolities and vicious international practices of others, was a fond hope of Americans—and like other fond hopes it soon went glimmering.

The first Americans accredited as envoys to European courts played the game much as they found it, padding com-

missions and setting up secret treaty clauses with all the skill
of fourth-generation experts. They were a talented lot, and
notable for their devotion to duty, their unswerving patriotism, and their brains. It is remarkable that the two most successful agents in this remarkable company, Benjamin Franklin and John Adams, were diplomatic opposites, the good
gray doctor being patient, suave, amiable, and understanding, while Adams, who infuriated all his associates, was
touchy, impatient, explosive, a screeching quarreler, monu-
mentally stubborn, and convinced at all times that God was
on his side.

Making war was easy; making peace was much more
difficult. For a long time before a treaty to put an end to the
fighting in America could be framed and implemented the
American ambassadors, early on the scene, found themselves
battling a succession of separatist proposals. None of these
was acceptable to the new nation, but each died hard. France
and the Netherlands, which were directly interested, and
Russia and Prussia and Austria, which weren't, all wanted
a say, all had ideas about how the thirteen American colonies
could be exquisitely torn apart, some to be granted independence, others to remain under the British crown. The
visitors from across the sea did not appreciate these efforts,
and their lack of appreciation was not enjoyed by the old-
time diplomatists, who saw nothing wrong with chopping up
the rest of the world as a housewife chops out cookies with
a cookie cutter.

It took a long time to assemble the peace of 1783 in
Paris, but the outcome was a triumph for the Americans, the
country cousins, who, themselves unhampered by the sticky
cobwebs of precedent, strove to take advantage of the con-
flicting squirts of spite on the part of others. Americans indeed got better terms than even they had expected. All
chance of keeping clear of the entangling political alliances
of Europe, however, had flown.

No sooner had this momentous piece of business been

completed when there burst upon the world another and much noisier revolution. It split the new nation in half.

There were those in the United States who cheered the French for doing what they thought Americans should have done while they were at it—that is, establish a truly democratic government. These people were to be found everywhere, but especially in the cities. They were seized with a patriotic frenzy. They believed that they were taking part in a world upheaval, and they burbled with joy. Liberty poles were erected, and topped with liberty caps. Tricolor cockades were seen everywhere, and men of advanced opinions took to wearing long trousers and coats with split tails, a sign of political emancipation. They greeted one another in the streets as "citizen" and even "citizeness." They sang *Ça Ira* and *La Marseillaise*. Starry-eyed, they drank toasts to *Liberté, Egalité, et Fraternité.*

Others, the crustier ones, the oldsters, shook their heads and clucked their tongues at this display of hysteria, and continued to wear knee breeches and stockings as their fathers and grandfathers had done. What, they asked, was the world coming to? The news of the Directorate and of the Reign of Terror gave substance to these complaints, but there were still many in America who persisted in believing that they stood upon a threshold; and these of course quoted the saying about the impossibility of making an omelette without breaking eggs.

Few of the leaders of the new nation favored the establishment of political parties, and most were vehemently opposed to this, the example of the British not being inspiriting. Nevertheless, and almost right away, there *were* two parties. The Federalists, centered upon New England, were, as their name implied, in favor of a strong central government. The republicans [29] professed to be strict interpreters of the new constitution. The leader of the republicans, tall gawky Thomas Jefferson, was fussily insistent upon this. He believed that Congress had only two kinds of powers: 1, those specifically delegated to it by the Constitution, and, 2, those necessary to carry the delegated powers into effect.

The first two Presidents, Washington and John Adams, were Federalists—though Washington would have liked to be thought above all faction. The real head of the party, however, was Alexander Hamilton, who had aristocratic ideas and was known to admire the British system of government. Jefferson, though his French leanings might have been exaggerated by his enemies, undoubtedly liked that country. He had been the United States minister to France, and a singularly sympathetic one, and he knew the language well and had many friends in France. Nor did the Terror frighten him, for had he not said that "the tree of liberty must be refreshed from time to time with the blood of patriots and tyrants"? He had added: "It is its natural manure."

Hamilton was wont to assert that the United States was an English-speaking nation, its background and its tradition, like its law, being English, while Jefferson would point out that it was France that had saved the struggling colonies with men and money when they needed these the most.

The Federalists thus were pro-English, the republicans pro-French. When Edmond Charles Genêt in 1793 was appointed by the French Directory as republican France's ambassador to the United States, this rift was to cause trouble.

Washington did not know what to do, and he called a meeting of his four-man cabinet. An orthodox military thinker in a day when no general would move without the approval and protection of a council of war, he was always quick to call cabinet meetings.

Should this representative of the regicides be received? Hamilton, secretary of the treasury, voted no. Jefferson, secretary of state, voted yes. The others (they were Henry Knox, secretary of war, and Edmund Randolph, attorney general: it was not the custom to have the vice-president sit in at cabinet meetings) didn't matter.

So here, this early, these archrivals faced one another

in contention. Their enmity was to change the nature of the land.

As usual, a compromise resulted. It was agreed to receive the oncoming ambassador, but to do so in the coldest manner possible.

There was another question at this cabinet meeting. Should the President issue a declaration of neutrality in the war that had broken out between France on one side, Great Britain, Spain, and the Netherlands on the other? He *wished* to issue such a declaration, but would it be proper? Jefferson opposed it, for two reasons. A strict constructionist, he contended that the Constitution gave Congress the right to declare war, and would not a declaration of neutrality, he asked, be the same thing as a declaration of war? Also, the United States was bound by the treaty of 1778 with France to assist her any time she was attacked. France had come into the Revolution, tipping the scales to victory, for that very reason. An injured friend, Jefferson pointed out, is the bitterest of foes.

Hamilton sneered at the neutrality-war differentiation as a splitting of hairs. As to the treaty of 1778, he said, it was made between the United States and the crown of France, which latter no longer existed as a political entity. Hamilton did not seem to think that *this* constituted a splitting of hairs. Moreover, Hamilton went on, with more cogency, France had not been attacked. *She* had attacked the others. *She,* and not Holland or Great Britain or Spain, had declared war.

Another compromise came out of this. A declaration would be issued, but, since Mr. Secretary Jefferson felt so strongly about it, the word "neutrality," which he found offensive, would not be used anywhere in it.

Genêt, when he came, came like a comet. Tall and handsome, fiery of speech (and he spoke seven languages), he was a fervent republican, convinced of the righteousness of his cause; and he was also a mathematician, an inventor, and a bold muddler of other people's politics.

Previous French ambassadors, the royal ones, Conrad Alexandre Gérard and the tubby persuasive Chevalier Anne-César De La Luzerne, had not hesitated to mix in the affairs of Congress, each controlling his own bloc, lecturing to invited groups of senators at the embassy, and otherwise indulging in meddlesome antics that would win any modern envoy his instant-departure papers. They were discreet compared with Genêt.

Charleston, South Carolina, in 1793 was crowded with Frenchmen, exiles from Haiti, where there had lately been a massive insurrection. It was at Charleston that Citizen Genêt landed, April 8. Philadelphia, the capital, was just as near to France and had as good a harbor. Genêt said that Charleston had been used because of adverse winds along the Philadelphia route, but nobody really believed this. He was out for the applause. His conveyance, the French frigate *l'Embuscade*, after a few days he sent on to Philadelphia anyway, and en route she picked up three British prizes, one of them inside the territorial waters of the United States.

Genêt himself spent eleven days in Charleston, wined and dined and repeatedly called upon to say a few words. He waved the tricolor exuberantly. He had in his bags three hundred blank privateering commissions, and he issued four of those right in Charleston, even though he had not yet been received by the President and his credentials examined. It took him twenty-eight days to go by land to Philadelphia, though he could have done it in three aboard the comfortable *l'Embuscade*. He stopped at every village where there was any sort of French colony, and his speeches, as always, were inflammatory. He put on a good show, but he seemed to suppose that the cheers it raised were directed at the cause he so passionately represented, and he grew giddy with the delusion of power.

When he heard that President Washington had issued a declaration of neutrality he canceled a speaking appointment at Fredericksburg, Maryland, and fairly flew to the capital.

TALL AND HANDSOME, FIERY OF SPEECH, EDMOND CHARLES GENÊT
WAS WINED AND DINED.

This was unspeakable! Why, America too was a republic, and she owed France many millions of dollars!

Everything that had gone before was as a murmur compared with the hoopla with which Philadelphia welcomed the visitor. Women rushed up to him and kissed him. Girls threw roses on, the pavement before him. All the bands played *La Marseillaise*.

With Washington it was different. President Washington, as planned, received him with a frosty correctitude. The Father of His Country was very good at that sort of thing. It did not faze Edmond Charles Genêt. Nothing fazed that man. As soon as Congress met again, he declared, it would be different. Congress was the real ruler of the nation, not General Washington, whom Citizen Genêt brushed aside as a petty despot, a would-be czar. This was his mistake, as he was to learn. The people loved and trusted George Washington, who was still alive and had not yet been frozen into a cold, cold statue.

Genêt's "war chest" was huge. He dipped into it again and again, commissioning French privateers, stirring up trouble in Nova Scotia and in Canada, and arranging for the organization of whole armies that were to be assigned to take New Orleans. There was nothing small about the man. His funds running short, he remembered that he was authorized, among other things, to collect, if he could, any part of the debt of the United States to France. He applied to the secretary of the treasury.

Hamilton said no. Hamilton indeed must have had a hard time forcing himself even to speak to Edmond Charles Genêt. Like Washington, Alexander Hamilton feared that if this illegal activity were permitted to continue it would mean that Great Britain would declare war on the United States, which could not stand such a thing.

Genêt was not dismayed. He still believed that the people of the United States were on his side and would support him, repudiating their President, when it came to a show-down.

Of the various rebellion plans that Genêt had in mind, the most ambitious was that for the seizure of New Orleans and later of both East and West Florida. His nation, humiliated in 1763 by Great Britain, was determined to return as an imperialist power in North America; and here was its opportunity. Genêt had started to work on it before he left Charleston, where one army was being formed to march into Tennessee and join with a larger Kentucky army before starting down the Mississippi. The Kentucky army and the eventually merged armies were to be commanded by that veteran western hero George Rogers Clark *if* Genêt could talk Clark into acceptance of the job.

Genêt need not have worried. When he got to Philadelphia he found waiting for him a letter from Clark, who, not waiting to be asked, proposed this very thing. The hero was getting restless with his laurels. Peace never had been a condition that he enjoyed.

Genêt agreed; and he commissioned George Rogers Clark a major general in the army of the French republic with the title "Commander in Chief of the Independent and Revolutionary Army of the Mississippi." More, Genêt authorized the Virginian to pay enlistees with land located in the Louisiana territory west of the Mississippi, for he assumed that this land would become France's once again as soon as New Orleans fell. Clark gleefully complied. He sometimes promised a private as much as three thousand acres, never less than one thousand, in addition to a share of the loot; and officers, of course, were to get more. Recruits poured in.

By this time even Thomas Jefferson was obliged to agree with Washington and Hamilton that matters had gone far enough, and as secretary of state he was about to ask France to recall its ambassador—when he learned that France already had done so.

Genêt had come like a comet, and like a comet he went.

Once the funds were cut off all his plans fell to earth, and the grand army that had started to form under George Rogers Clark simply dissolved, its members going home.

There had been a change of government in Paris. The Girondists, Genêt's party, were out, and the slavering, bloodthirsty Jacobins were in, and one of the first things that the Jacobins did was appoint a new ambassador to the United States, instructing him when he got there to send Genêt back.

Genêt was no fool. He knew what this meant. It meant that they wanted his head over there, literally. He dropped all his grandiose schemes of revolution and applied to the United States government for political asylum, which was granted—the first such case in the history of America. Genêt married a Clinton, daughter of the governor of New York, very rich; and he lived happily—and quietly, non-politically—forever after.

The mouth of the Mississippi remained in Spanish hands.

10

A Tale of Two Treaties

CARLOS IV OF SPAIN succeeded his father, Carlos III, late in 1788, his older brother having been passed over as an imbecile. The old man had been caustic, frugal, fussy, intensely religious. The son also was religious. When his cousins of France proposed that with some spare northern Italian provinces they had recently overrun they would form a new kingdom, giving the throne thereof to the young Duke of Parma, Carlos's son-in-law, he seemed at first delighted. The new place would be called Etruria, after the ancient land, and it would consist of three thrown-together duchies containing more than a million inhabitants in northern Italy, approximately the present Tuscany. This would make King Carlos's beloved daughter a queen. It would certainly please his own wife, who was herself a Parma. All France asked in return was the retrocession of Louisiana, a losing business at best. Yet when Carlos learned that the three provinces all had been wrested from the Pope he demurred, angrily. He would not take property that belonged to the Pope! What did they think he was?

As a youth, Carlos IV, a giant, used to go about the

countryside wrestling with the strongest men he could find. When he grew up he had only two pastimes. He was a locksmith or gunsmith, assuredly a blacksmith, and was never so happy as when toiling at his forge, unless it was when he was hunting. Hundreds of men, literally, assisted him in the hunt, but the king himself did all the actual shooting. He was called the best shot in Europe. Yet he killed only animals, never any of his wife's lovers.

It is conceivable that he never *knew* about his wife's lovers, although everybody else did. Though not a certifiable lunatic, like his brother, Carlos wasn't notably bright. He had an exalted sense of his duty as a God-created monarch, and it could be that his dignity prevented him from showing any awareness of what was going on around the palace whenever he wasn't home. His closest associates and friends, if he could be said to have any friends, were never sure of this.

It was certain that the blacksmith-king always pretended that he was, by inheritance, all-powerful; he refused to acknowledge the lackey's position his country had been forced to assume under the so-called Family Compact; and it may have been the same with his marriage.

The first of the male Pompadours at Madrid, and the best of them, was Don Manuel Luis de Godoy, a well-built young guardsman—he was twenty-five when the Queen's eye first fell upon him—who, overnight, had become prime minister. Godoy, though new in the part, and with no political experience, had done much to bring about the end of an expensive war with France by means of the treaty of Basle, after which the amused public had hailed him as the Prince of Peace. It was something more than a mere nickname, and he liked it. He had a title of his own, one of the first things her Majesty had arranged for—he was the Duke of Alcudia, but he preferred to be addressed as Your Highness. He had been penniless a little while ago, but now suddenly he was very rich; and even after he had ceased to be the royal paramour he remained—like Potemkin with Catherine of Russia—

the Queen's best friend and favorite counselor and the head of the government. He was unfailingly considerate of his successors. The king, too, liked him and trusted him: they were often together.

To most Americans, who were only vaguely aware of these Gomorrhean goings-on, the Prince of Peace must have seemed despicable, crawly, a thing not to be touched even with a stick. Yet he was to prove one of the best friends the United States ever had.

Three-fourths of the trade of the new republic was with Great Britain, and only about one-seventh with France, as the secretary of the treasury pointed out to President Washington early in his first term of office. By far the biggest part of the income of the United States was made up of import duties, mostly on British goods. It would be well, then, Hamilton pursued, if we had a commercial treaty with that country. Instead, we were on the edge of war with her. The secretary of state, Mr. Jefferson, had repeatedly asked the British government to evacuate the various forts of the Northwestern Territory, as called upon to do by the treaty of 1783, but he no longer even got an answer. The current United States minister at Whitehall, Thomas Pinckney, was only that, a minister. Hamilton proposed to his boss that a full-fledged ambassador be sent there, equipped with both extraordinary *and* plenipotentiary powers. Washington agreed.

There was some mention of Hamilton himself for the post. He was not a man to be averse to holding down two or three jobs at the same time; but here he said no. He had too many enemies in the Senate, he said. His nomination never would be ratified. John Jay was named instead. The Senate did consent to this, though reluctantly and by a narrow vote. Jay was chief justice of the United States.

They must have made a curious pair, as Jay took over. Pinckney the planter was from South Carolina, Jay the lawyer, from New York. Both were rich, both Federalists, but

JOHN JAY—GRUFF, BEETLEBROWED, LANK, SUSPICIOUS

Thomas Pinckney was elegant, a model of deportment, suave, plump, a dandy, whereas the gruff John Jay was a scarecrow in appearance, beetlebrowed, lank, suspicious.

They got along well together. Pinckney had every right to be sore about being so abruptly replaced, but he acceded with a smile. He had lived half his life in England, and had been educated there—Westminster, Oxford—so that he knew his way around. He saw that John Jay met the right people, though he must have known that if a treaty was framed Jay would get all the credit—or, as it happened in this case, the blame. Pinckney even co-operated in the framing; and after that he was dispatched to Madrid as United States ambassador, this time with full plenipotentiary *and* extraordinary powers.

The Jay Treaty almost tore their home nation apart. Nobody liked it; and most Americans were red with indignation about it. Supercilious England, it did seem, was deliberately rubbing the noses of her late colonies in the dust. There *was* an agreement that the northwestern forts be evacuated, true; but in payment for this England exacted commercial limitations that emphasized her claim to be Mistress of the Seas.

England's excuse, if for an instant she had granted that she needed one, would have been that she was engaged in war. There was of course nothing unusual about that; but *this* war looked to be for keeps.

The armies of the French Revolution seemed determined to cram their *Liberté, Egalité, Fraternité* down the throat of every nation they could lay hands on. At first they had struck at Prussia and Austria, countries not notable for their seagoing trade; but more recently they had declared war against the Netherlands, Great Britain, and Spain, all commercial countries with which the affairs of the new United States were inextricably connected. This was no token conflict for diplomats seated around a baize-covered table. This was a combat *à outrance*, to the death. The United States, whether or not it wanted to—and it most certainly did *not* want to—had to choose sides; and in accordance with the recommendation of Alexander Hamilton, and in view of the balance of trade, it chose Great Britain. Knowing that it would do so, Great Britain turned the screws . . . and turned them . . .

Jay had done the best he could, but the result was hardly a thing to cause joy in America. President Washington himself liked Jay's Treaty so little that he held on to it for four months before he ventured to submit it to the Senate, where it was sure to be roughly handled. The country roared with rage, and there was a great deal of talk about a second revolution.

The Senate ratified the thing by one vote. Meanwhile the House of Representatives had taken it up as an emergency measure, though President Washington warned it that under the new Constitution it had no business to do so. It debated the treaty for more than a month, and at last passed favorably upon it by a majority of three. Washington proclaimed it February 2, 1796; but nobody was happy.

John Jay, for the moment the most hated man in America, resigned from the Supreme Court and went back to private law practice in New York.

Jay had spent two miserable years in Spain as an accredited ambassador who was not recognized by the court as such, and had got nowhere, a frustrating experience. This had been near the end of the War of the Revolution, and though Spain was a participant she did not approve of her nominal ally, the struggling young republic. In fact, Spain did not approve of republics at all, of any fashion, and was especially fearful of the emergence of one in America, where it might give ideas of liberty to some of Spain's manacled colonies.

No doubt Jay warned Thomas Pinckney of this. But the situation had changed. When Jay was in Madrid the Spanish court had not yet acknowledged the sovereignty of the United States, though technically an ally of that country. Now, in 1795, when Pinckney went to Madrid, nobody could possibly deny that sovereignty. Moreover, Spain was jealous of Great Britain and hoped to hurt her by befriending her enemy.

"There never was a good war, or a bad peace," is attributed to Benjamin Franklin. Nobody would dispute the first part; but there has been more than one bad peace. There was the peace that in 1763, for instance, ended the Seven Years' War. In this the victor, Great Britain, was so inconscionably voracious, grabbing huge chunks of territory all over the world, always at the expense of the loser, France, that France never forgave. The ink was not dry on the signatures to this treaty before France was beginning preparations for the next war. It was because of this, and not for any emotional attachment to the rebels, that France agreed to help the thirteen American colonies in their struggle against Great Britain, a help that made victory certain; and because of this, too, Spain had been dragged into the contest.

When he sat down to discuss business with Thomas Pinckney, the Prince of Peace, it is believed, had not seen a copy of the Jay Treaty,[30] but he certainly knew in a rough way what it would contain. The United States would be publicly humiliated, as France had been: this was certain. A good word for the new American nation would do at least a little to temper the arrogance of Albion, who, though technically an ally actually was a menace to Spain in the New World. Godoy knew this; and he was prepared to be cooperative. Half of Pinckney's work had been done for him before he left London.

There was hardly any haggling. Despite the dirty trick that America had played in consenting to the secret clause in the treaty that ended her war with Great Britain, Spain immediately granted that the northern boundary of both Floridas should be fixed at 31 degrees, instead of 32 degrees, 30 minutes, as she had previously claimed.

Thomas Jefferson as secretary of state lately had issued a white paper setting forth the idea that since the ocean is free to all nations of the world so should the rivers be free, and if the rivers were free in any one part they should be free from source to mouth. In support of this he had quoted Grotius, Vattel, Pufendorf, and other respectable thinkers. These were not authorities who commanded any respect in Spain; and the white paper changed nothing.[31] Nevertheless, Manuel de Godoy, the Prince of Peace, on this occasion was to declare himself, inferentially, to be of Thomas Jefferson's way of thinking.

Article XXII of the new treaty read:

And, in consequence of the stipulations contained in the fourth article, his Catholic Majesty will permit the citizens of the United States, for the space of three years from this time, to deposit their merchandises and effects in the port of New Orleans, and to export them from thence without paying any other duty than a fair price for the hire of the stores; and his Majesty promises either to continue this permission, if he finds, during that time, that it is not prejudicial to the interests of Spain; or if he should not agree to continue it there, he will assign to them, on another part of the banks of the Mississippi, an equivalent establishment.

Was this a grant? or was it the recognition of a right? Pinckney himself was not sure, though he knew that future generations might hang on the definition. He tried, to clear the matter, to get written into this article: "It is nevertheless agreed, that nothing contained in this article shall be construed or interpreted, to communicate the right of navigating this river to other nations or persons, than to the subjects of His Catholic Majesty, and to the citizens of the United States." He failed in this. Godoy had gone far enough.

The thing was done, and it was a triumph, a bright jewel in the diadem of American diplomacy. John Jay's failure had brought about the dazzling success of Thomas Pinckney. Dislike of England had scored again, and scored tellingly. The treaty called for ratifications within six months of the time of signing, which was furiously fast in view of the communications of the time. Yet it was made, with a few days to spare. The United States Senate never hesitated, but passed upon the treaty with a whoop, without a dissenting vote. Ratifications were exchanged, in Spain, April 25, 1796.

The Mississippi at last was open—forever.

Or so it seemed.

11

What Happened to a Truculent Quaker

THE CREOLES OF NEW ORLEANS, who did not like him, called Carondelet, the new governor, "Cochon de Lait." This was never very funny; it was not accurate; and it is doubtful that the governor ever heard of it anyway, for he was busy getting things done.

He was aghast at the conditions as he had found them in the Crescent City, where a largely French populace was growling threats of rebellion while their countrymen at home increased the pressure for a retrocession of the whole territory. The accursed Kaintucks kept filtering into the Creek and Chickasaw country to the north and east, and kept pouring down the mighty Mississippi, always with the air of conquerors. The Baron de Carondelet had fewer than two thousand soldiers with whom to defend his line from the mouth of the big river clear up to St. Louis, and not many of these were regulars, the greater part being unskilled and poorly disciplined militiamen. His artillery pieces were ancient and undependable, his powder supply low. His forts were mere pillboxes.

He did have a strong second-in-command, Manuel Gayoso de Lemos, who was in charge of the Natchez district. Gayoso was a bon vivant, famous for the cellar he kept, but he was also a shrewd administrator, and he could speak excellent English, an asset for a man who would be the first important Spanish official the oncoming Kaintucks would meet. The governor himself had not a word of English.

Carondelet also had General Wilkinson, a man he never met. The "Spanish Conspiracy" had seemed for a short while to slumber, but recently it had come back to life. Major General George Rogers Clark, clad in the resplendent authority conferred upon him by Citizen Genêt, had been a whirlwind of activity in the valley of the Ohio, recruiting men, instructing officers, allotting land, accumulating supplies, arranging for boats. Of all this preparation James Wilkinson, commander-in-chief of the United States Army, had been careful to keep the governor of Louisiana informed; for Wilkinson was a conscientious agent.

Then came Secretary Hamilton's refusal to pay back before it was due any of the money the United States had borrowed from France; and the political overturn in Paris, and the appointment of a new ambassador to the United States; so that all Genêt's plans collapsed, as did General Clark's, which had been dependent upon French gold.

Wilkinson had reported all this to his employers, after which he sent them an itemized bill for $8,640 expenses. Wilkinson always did have a heavy hand with an expense account.

Wilkinson gave advice as well. It was his suggestion that the Spaniards fortify Chickasaw Bluffs, an easily defended spot some 155 miles upriver from Natchez on the east bank of the Mississippi.[32] This was done.

Carondelet lowered the tariff on northern goods from 15 percent to 6 percent. He would encourage the Kaintucks, whom he believed, largely on the basis of Wilkinson's reports, were again ready to break away from the federal union.

When Wilkinson proposed that the governor establish a

fund of $200,000 for the purpose of keeping certain Kentucky "notables" (whom Wilkinson listed) happy, Carondelet snatched at the idea. Madrid, however, spoke an icy no. Louisiana was costing too much already. Carondelet must be mad, asking for such sums. The subject was dropped.

Still infatuated with his informant, Carondelet sent one Thomas Power, an American, to Wilkinson with his pension for that year. Power was instructed to urge the separation plot upon General Wilkinson, who could then call himself the Washington of the West, an enticing title. Now, however, the general was coy. Though Kentucky recently had been granted statehood, secession sentiment remained strong —but seemingly not strong enough to satisfy James Wilkinson, who after all would be jeopardizing a good job. He declined to act, at least right then and there. Nevertheless the pension was kept up.

News of the Pinckney Treaty—in history it is the Treaty of San Lorenzo el Real, but to Americans it will always be the Pinckney—must have struck Governor Carondelet with stunning force. Now *he* thought that *Madrid* had gone mad. Without any warning, without having been giving an idea of what was cooking in the diplomatic pot, he was ordered to give up all his posts on the east bank of the Mississippi above New Orleans. Baton Rouge, Natchez, Nogales, Chickasaw Bluffs—all must go. It was a pill hard to swallow.

Article III of this incredible treaty provided that each signatory should appoint "one Commissioner and one surveyor," all four to meet at Natchez "before the expiration of six months from the ratification of this convention, and they shall proceed to run and mark this boundary according to the stipulations of the said Article." Precautions were taken against the possibility that one side might try to "jump" the other. If "on any account it should be found necessary that the said Commissioners and Surveyors should be accompanied by Guards," the article went on, "these should be provided in equal numbers for each side," presumably against Indian attacks. It was all very well to lay down such conditions in a palace in Madrid, but could they be made to work in the wilderness?

The American commissioner appeared with disconcerting promptitude, popping up in Natchez. His name was Andrew Ellicott, and his nature was scrappy, his temper hair-triggered. He was a Quaker, but bellicose. He bristled.

The governor simply had not been able to believe the news of the Treaty of San Lorenzo el Real; and at first he thought—he could devise no other explanation—that this information should have been accompanied by secret orders telling him to disregard it and to hold onto the forts at all costs. This secret order, he supposed, had gone astray. It was the sort of thing that happened all the time. He wrote to Madrid asking for clarification, and meanwhile he prepared to put off the American surveyors. Posts up the river were notified, in case they came from the Ohio valley country, posts down the river in case they tried to come up from the Gulf. Officials were to be polite, of course; but they were to find reasons—any reasons—for holding up the party.

Carondelet conferred with Gayoso. They agreed that the Chickasaw and the Upper Creeks surely would have caused trouble if the Spanish forts along the east bank of the Mississippi were dismantled, so that any American surveying team in those parts would be in danger—something that would have been news to the Creeks and the Chickasaw. If only the delay was made to hold until the end of the year, Gayoso and Carondelet perceived, they could point out to the Americans that the movement of the artillery—taking the guns from Chickasaw Bluffs up to St. Louis on the other bank, for example—would have to be postponed until the high water of spring. Meanwhile, it was hoped that some word would come from Madrid.

Ellicott came downstream. He was delayed at New Madrid, Chickasaw Bluffs, Walnut Hills, but never for long. To hold him they would have had to fight him, and nobody wanted that.

Ellicott had about twenty soldiers with him, under the command of a Lieutenant Pope, known to his men, semi-affectionately, as Crazy Pope. Gayoso had almost fifty at Natchez when at last they met face to face.

The pugnacious Mr. Ellicott proposed that he start work on that surveying job right away. Gayoso, turning on his charm, suggested a relaxing trip to New Orleans first. It was an interesting place, New Orleans. Ellicott said no.

Gayoso offered a drink. Ellicott said that he didn't drink.

Ellicott took over the building assigned to him and his men, and started to strengthen its walls. Also, he planted a flagpole, upon which he ran up the Stars and Stripes. Gayoso, always the gentleman, asked him please not to keep that flag there: after all, this was still Spanish territory, and it might cause trouble among his men. Ellicott replied that the flag would stay.

The situation was further complicated by the fact that both sides knew that France for some time had been angling to lift the Louisiana territory out of the international pond, and that even while this tongue-sticking show was in progress at Natchez a French general, Victor Collot, was making a full military survey of the whole valley. In other words, if the prickly stubbornness of Andrew Ellicott should bring about a war between the United States and Spain—and wars have been touched off by less—it might at any moment mean that Spain meant France as well, which could result in the trampling to death of the weak new republic. Nevertheless Ellicott persisted.

His little thrown-together fort sat upon one hill; and less than a mile away, atop another hill, was the Spanish fort. Gayoso ordinarily kept his calm, but once in a pet he ordered a cannon at the Spanish stronghold to be loaded and shotted and aimed directly upon the other fort. Nothing happened. The Stars and Stripes still waved.

Ellicott was not helped by those under him. Crazy Pope was notoriously unpredictable. The privates, like virtually all privates in the United States Army at the time, were riffraff, irresponsible. Moreover, Ellicott's chief assistant, his surveyor, Thomas Freeman, had a habit of getting drunk in public and drawing his sword and waving it over his head, while at the top of his lungs he recited Shakespeare. Natchez in those days was a very bad town to get drunk in.

Not Freeman, however, but one Hanna, an itinerant Baptist preacher who was a hanger-on at Ellicott's camp, came closest to bringing about a clash. Hanna got drunk, probably on taffia, a low grade of rum, and went over to Gayoso and cursed him. The Spaniard ordered him thrown into jail, and this was done.

Instantly Andrew Ellicott was on the other hill, and raging. "Release that man," he cried, "or else—!"

Hanna was released.

Eventually, and after a great deal of prevarication, the Americans, who had finished their work in the vicinity of Natchez, were permitted to set about drawing the long line through the wilderness. This they did, and they did it well. There were no further clashes. The job took several years, and so quietly did it end that in retrospect the beginnings of the task were touched with comic-opera tints; and history, when it notices Ellicott's expedition at all, inclines to dismiss it with a chuckle, calling it the Quaker Victory.

The Spanish forts at last were demolished, and the land on which they stood was formally turned over to army officers, subalterns of General Wilkinson, who watched with benign approval. All Spanish troops were not evacuated from the territory "within six months or sooner," as provided in the Treaty of San Lorenzo el Real, but they *were* evacuated.

Traffic increased on the river. More English was heard

at Natchez, at Baton Rouge, and New Orleans. The republic —it had a population of a little over 5,000,000, almost one-fifth of them black slaves, as compared with 15,000,000 for Great Britain, 27,000,000 for France—as it approached the end of the century, though it was shaky, and quivered with internal dissension, somehow held itself together. Its people looked toward a better day. They placed great faith in Thomas Jefferson, the new President.

12

His Heart Was Out-of-Doors

LIKE ALEXANDER MCGILLIVRAY, here was an improbable hero. Jefferson was tall, but of unimpressive aspect. He was shy, and couldn't make a speech worth listening to. He was gawky, all arms and legs. His clothes looked too small for him.

He got things done not by pounding the table, not by speechifying, nor by scolding his followers as he organized them in lobbies and cloakrooms. He did not even write pamphlets or editorials for newspapers, though he was the possessor of a smooth and flexible literary style. He got things done—and he *did* get them done—very largely by writing letters to his friends. No one was in doubt as to where Thomas Jefferson stood, unless it was, sometimes, for a little while, Thomas Jefferson. Never smug, he yet radiated serenity.

This widower had sandy red hair, which he refused to powder, as he refused to wear a wig. Any sort of formality frightened him, and he barred protocol from the White House. Louis XIV, the Sun King, sometimes received ambassadors whilst defecating. President Jefferson never went

THE YOUNG REPUBLIC, SHAKY AND QUIVERING WITH INTERNAL DIS-
SENSION, PLACED GREAT FAITH IN THOMAS JEFFERSON, THE NEW
PRESIDENT.

that far, but he did receive them in bedroom slippers. The French have an expression, *en pantoufles*, meaning wearing such slippers—that is, at home, off guard, with the hair down. Such an expression never could have been applied to Thomas Jefferson, though he admired the French and was greatly admired by them. He was always that way—usually, literally, *en pantoufles*.

He succeeded Benjamin Franklin as United States ambassador to France; and Franklin's, as they say in show business, was a hard act to follow. The French took to Jefferson, however, despite his *gaucherie*, his lack of polish. For the man was a thinker, a dreamer even. He was an architect, a scientist. Not only had he written the Declaration of Independence, but he had first advanced the idea for the University of Virginia, which he plotted in its entirety and designed. He was the first to propose the establishment of the Library of Congress, and his own private library almost certainly was the biggest and the best in America. He invented the dumbwaiter. He built Monticello. He, the first again, warned against "entangling alliances" with European nations. He played several musical instruments. He was honestly and intensely concerned with the welfare of his fellow men. He hated war.

Many of those who did not hate war but indeed made a profession of it were quick to accuse Thomas Jefferson of walking around with his head in the clouds. This was especially true of the big-navy men, who liked to think of themselves as hard-boiled realists. In the United States the big-navy men have traditionally looked upon those who differed from them, who believed in looking at the price first, as weaklings, cowards, as shortsighted and unpatriotic fools, and they have never hesitated to say so. Jefferson was not to be immune to this kind of slander. It did not seem to trouble him. He took up the struggle against the Barbary pirates left to him by his predecessor, John Adams, and after greatly strengthening the United States Navy he carried that struggle to a successful conclusion. Afterward he would have saved the taxpayers immense sums of money, while still keeping the navy more or less in service, by putting the idle frigates high in special drydocks, equipped with dehumidifiers, which he himself was prepared to design. This proposal (it was never to be tried) caused the big-navy men to guffaw unrestrainedly, slapping their knees; yet it was a clear foreshadowing of the United States Navy's current "mothball" program.

That Jefferson was in fact realistic in his attitude toward international policy, and that he did not despise England as his enemies said, is proved by a letter he wrote April 18, 1802, to Robert Livingston, the United States ambassador to France:

> There is on the globe one single spot the possessor of which is our natural and habitual enemy. It is New Orleans. The day that France takes possession of New Orleans fixes the sentence which is to restrain her within her low water mark. From that day we must marry ourselves to the British fleet and nation.

Most of the first settlers west of the mountains had been southerners, but since the Revolution more and more of them had been coming from New England and the middle Atlantic states. Yet to a man, almost, they were in favor of Jefferson. Why?

He was a Virginia gentleman, a planter, a slave owner. He was an intellectual, and customarily moved among exalted friends. So far from being outgoing, a back slapper, a user of first names, he was shy, retiring; he was bookish. He had never, himself, crossed the mountains. He had no financial interests there, no business connections. Yet they believed in him. Why?

They did not get his letters. None of them had heard him speak, and very few could even have glimpsed him from afar.

His sloppiness might have had something to do with it. Westerners would have applauded his giving up of knee breeches and silk stockings, and they would have been amused to hear about his receiving foreign dignitaries in his bedroom slippers, in an old dressing robe, and about his enforcement at the White House of what he called the rule of *pêle-mêle*, by which guests went in to dinner in any old order and with any convenient partner, regardless of rank. The westerners enjoyed that sort of thing.

More likely they sensed the sincerity of this patriot, his unconquerable goodwill. He favored the small man, the tiller of his own soil. He might mix with the elite, but westerners believed that inherently he was one of their own kind. He had no use for the cities, with their dirt, their stink, and the pauseless jangle of their money. His heart was out-of-doors.

Jefferson never affected the "homespun" dress, speech, and manners that were to become the stock in trade of many a western politician and especially those from the South. He didn't drawl. He did not tell folksy stories. It seemed that he was instinctively with those people on the far side of the mountains; he understood them and needed no costume to wear when he mingled with them.

Regrettable as it might seem to the founding fathers, the emergence of a two-party system in America did cause men to look at issues rather than leaders, at least for a little while, and to examine the underlying philosophy of those who sat in the seats of power. The westerners immediately favored the republican-democratic concept rather than that of the Federalists. Once Washington had retired to private life this split was sure to become a deciding factor in national affairs. The first post-Washington presidential election, that of 1796, had been very close: seventy-one electoral votes for John Adams, the Federalist, to sixty-eight for Jefferson. Thereafter the Federalist cause went steadily and swiftly downhill, though the party did for some time retain control of Congress. In 1800 the Federalists were all but wiped out in the electoral college, and the Presidency wavered between two republican candidates, Thomas Jefferson and Aaron Burr, who had received an equal number of electoral votes. This, as the Constitution stood then,[33] put the choice up to the House of Representatives, still controlled by the lame-duck Federalists. The deadlock continued for some months, as both candidates refused to make promises to the Federalists, who understandably tried to take advantage of their position. It was finally decided, by *one* vote, in favor of Jefferson.

The Federalist idea of an all-powerful central government did not appeal to the easygoing, independent westerners, with their fondness for segmenting into small separate states at the slimmest excuse. It was Jefferson's protégé, James Madison, who had written the celebrated Virginia Resolutions of 1798, and Jefferson himself, who, a little later that same year, had written the even more famous and even more outspoken Kentucky Resolutions, which began:

> *Resolved,* that the several States composing the United States of America, are not united on the principle of unlimited submission to their general government . . . That the government created by this compact was not made the exclusive or final judge of the extent of the powers delegated to itself; since that would have made its discretion, and not the Constitution, the measure of its powers; but that as in all other cases of compact among parties having no common Judge, each party has an equal right to judge for itself, as well of infractions as of the mode and measure of redress.

This was language the westerner could understand.

Then there was the matter of France. The Federalists insisted that Jefferson was too sympathetic toward France, though it was said of *them*, in turn, that they were too sympathetic toward Great Britain. Westerners had no fondness for foreigners of any kind, but a fact that could not be avoided was the fact that whichever nation controlled the mouth of the Mississippi River controlled the whole Mississippi Valley. That nation, ostensibly, was Spain, which could be bullied into compliance with the wishes of the westerners. But how long would Spain remain the country in control? Wasn't it almost sure to become France again, and very soon?

(In fact, the Treaty of San Ildefonso, which gave back to France not only New Orleans but also the whole of the Louisiana Territory, was signed April 30, 1800. It was supposed to be a secret, but the secret was not well kept, and, though Spanish officials in Louisiana continued to perform their functions, anybody who was interested knew or strongly suspected that France could take over any time she wished.)

Jefferson liked the French, but there was no reason to suppose that he loved them. He spoke their language, and it could be assumed that he understood them, if anybody did, and could cope with their queer changes of character.

The situation in France was confused. Writers of diplomatic papers continued to refer to France as a republic, its official designation, but in truth it was nothing of the sort, nor had it been since the coup d'état of November 9–10, 1799, when the old and bloody Directorate was overthrown. In the course of that momentous event there came to the top, mysteriously, a short, swart army officer from Corsica named Napoleon Bonaparte; and nothing in Europe was ever to be the same again.

Bonaparte was only the First Consul of France, but nobody could remember the names of the Second or Third. He was, almost immediately, supreme. Today it is hard to see why. There was nothing attractive about him; and indeed he was a cold, forbidding, fishlike person of notably bad temper, pettish, and anything but handsome. He was unaccountable, undependable, not even a Frenchman. He was a good soldier, at times even a brilliant one, but he was not a great general, and gave nothing tellingly new to the military art, as did Gustavus Adolphus with his second line, Marlborough with his holding attack, Frederick the Great with the horse artillery. Napoleon won, when he won, because of superior numbers swiftly and crushingly employed with no counting of the cost. He was a butcher. His dependence was upon massive armies, raised by conscription, used like so many steam rollers. Even so, it is to be noted that he lost as many campaigns as he won, and that he was to lose the most important battle of all, the last.

Bonaparte bewildered the emergent America quite as much as he bewildered Europe. Men just never *did* learn what to expect from him. He could desert his trusted companions whenever his own skin or his military reputation was at stake, as he had deserted Paoli in Corsica, and all his generals, all his faithful men too, in Egypt, leaving them to their fate while he sneaked home to mend political fences; yet whenever he rode out the troops cheered him. He could keep his own counsel until the last moment, when he would suddenly do the unexpected, the spectacular. It was known of him only that he had a very low explosive point, and that his rages were terrible. Once, screeching, he called Charles Maurice de Talleyrand-Périgord, *"La merde dans un bas de soie,"* and that iridescent, inscrutable statesman was heard to mutter afterward, whilst shaking his head, "What a pity that so great a man should have such bad manners!"

Perhaps here was the answer? As the politenesses of traditional diplomats must be finger-sorted with care in order to find, if there were any, fragments of the truth, so, it could be, must the rudenesses of this bad-tempered little dictator. It was possible that he had reversed not only the matter but the whole *manner* of intercommunication among the rulers of the world, and that in future, at least in France, not sugar pills but gall and wormwood would make up the customary diplomatic dosage.

Trembling ambassadors asked one another: *Could* Bonaparte be as irascible, as egotistic, and cruel, as he seemed? Could *any* man?

They were soon to learn.

13

They Left by the Back Door

Bacon and salted pork went down the river, and grindstones and millstones, and jerked beef, kitchenware, anvils, shovels, whiskey, flour, cornmeal, also beaver skins, coonskins, the pelts of wildcats and of otter, beeswax, buffalo meat, butter, flints, ginseng, sawn planks, and more whiskey. Some few of these were sold in the settlements of the Natchez-Manchac district, some were sold in New Orleans, but most went out of the country by means of the country's back door, the mouth of the Mississippi.

The intendant at New Orleans did once, briefly, prohibit the delivery of whiskey to the Crescent City. He said that he did this for moral reasons—the stuff was ruining the character of the creoles, he declared—but everybody knew that it was really done in order to help the local rum people. Whiskey was easily smuggled in, however, and the ban didn't last long.

As the eighteenth century drew toward its close, the economy of Louisiana province, always a losing proposition, began to pick up a bit. Louisiana tobacco, never very good, had been banned by the government of Spain, by law its only

117

possible market. Despite the fond predictions of the late John Law, there seemed to be no mineral deposits to develop. Three-fourths of the population and seven-eighths of the wealth of Louisiana lay below Point Coupée at the mouth of the Red River; and the economy drooped even there. In 1792 an insect plague had wiped out the indigo crop. It looked as though Louisiana was finished.

Then, less than two years after the plague, a young Connecticut schoolteacher over in Georgia, where he was visiting his friend, the widow of General Nathanael Greene, the Revolutionary hero, invented a contraption that would take the seeds out of long-staple cotton as quickly and thoroughly as a whole shedful of slaves. Eli Whitney patented this device in 1794, and he and his partner, who financed him, hoped to make a fortune out of it; but the thing was so simple that it was readily imitated, or stolen, and in a little while it was all over the South, and the planters were not paying any royalties. Louisiana, too, took to cotton.

At about the same time the infant cane-sugar industry in those parts began to stir and to stretch itself. The local rum, of course, was a by-product of the sugar.

This comparative prosperity was reflected in the tolerance shown for the through-river traffic. Pinckney's Treaty had granted the right of deposit at New Orleans for only three years, but when that time had expired, in 1798, nobody even commented upon the circumstance. The grant was not renewed, but the shipments rolled on. It looked as though good times had come to stay.

To move this freight, at least as far south as the Crescent City, there evolved a new type of humanity, the river man. He was a hard case, with muscles of steel, damn-you eyes, and a monumental thirst. Like the later and longer-lived cowboy he toiled long and valiantly at a dirty, monotonous job, for which he was paid peanuts; and he romped—whenever he was allowed to romp for a little while—violently.

There never had been anything like the Mississippi River boat hand before, and there never will be anything like him again.

The first ones were French, and they were few in number. They were a carefree, clamorous lot, men in moccasins and fringed buckskin trousers, and with blue surtouts that fell to the knees, taken up at the waist with bright red woolen sashes. Sometimes too they wore bright red stocking-hats. They could endure almost anything, and they loved to sing. They called themselves *mangeurs de lard*, pork eaters, for bacon was a staple in their diet. When they got to New Orleans they mixed naturally with the crowd, and not many of them even thought of going back.

The Kaintucks came soon afterward. When they worked, which was most of the time, the Kaintucks worked hard, poling, rowing, or holding onto a bucking steering oar, in all sorts of weather. Off duty they were rambunctious, rampageous, rough.

> Hard upon the beech oar—
> She moves too slow!
> All the way to Shawneetown,
> Long while ago.

They had their songs, which they did not call chanties. They often implored the Buffalo Gals to come out, and they were to boast that they could "Dance all night till broad daylight / And go home with the girls in the morning," though most of what dancing they were able to do must have been stag style, like that of the early miners in the California gold rush, for women were few and far between in those parts.

The boatmen of the Mississippi were not running away from anything. They were not fugitives from justice, or debtors, or simple misfits. They took those long arduous trips because they liked the life of the river. It was a young man's game. If one of them was over thirty-five he was inevitably called Pappy.

Sometimes an entire family manned a raft or boat, in which case the chain of command was as it always had been at home, but such voyages customarily were short ones, and the full Ohio-Mississippi trips were usually made by professionals, full-timers. The leader or captain was called the patroon. He was hired directly by the owner, and was himself sometimes a part owner of the vessel or the cargo. When they were under way his word was absolute, his decisions final. When the craft was tied up at a town he prudently stayed out of the way of the hands, who of course got drunk. There were no other officers, no sort of assistant overseer, even on the larger vessels. Seldom was there a passenger.

The crew might consist of as few as three or as many as thirty. They were a close-knit group while afloat, for the patroon kept them busy, but on land they might fight freely among themselves—if there was nobody else to fight with.

Fighting indeed was their favorite occupation. There occasionally was a knife thrower in the crew, or a card sharp, who might keep the boys amused for a little while when they were ashore at a bar; and some, too, were crack shots who loved to show off. Mike Fink, called the King of the Keelboatmen, might summon his woman, if he had brought one along, and have her hitch up her skirt to the thighs and place a full cup of whiskey between her knees; then Mike would shoot the cup out, the length of the barroom away. Or, the woman not being present, such a tin cup would be placed on top of a friend's head, where Mike would shoot a hole through it so that the whiskey trickled down the man's face. Once Mike missed and shot a model right between the eyes, and a friend of *that* man, who didn't believe Mike's story that his hand had slipped, shot and killed Mike, thus putting an end to a legend comparable to the legends that

MIKE FINK WAS KNOWN AS ONE OF THE BEST RIFLE SHOTS ON THE RIVERS. From *The Great West*, 1847. *Courtesy, Saint Louis Mercantile Library Association*

clustered around John Henry of the hammer and Paul Bunyan the lumberjack.

Songs were written about Mike Fink, and innumerable stories were told, all of them tall. He was of the stuff of which myths are made; yet he was no shining Sunday School character! That woman from between whose knees he would shoot the cup, for instance, appears to have been different

MIKE FINK, KING OF THE KEELBOATMEN. From *The Crockett Almanac*, 1838. *Courtesy, Saint Louis Mercantile Library Association*

each time, and nobody ever did contend that she was Mike's *wife,* if he had one. Also, it was said of him that when the going was easy on the river, and the hands for the moment had no work, Mike, lolling, with his rifle would pick off stray Indians or Negro field hands along the shore, just for laughs.

The fist fight, however, was the greatest attraction. It seldom developed into a free-for-all, for the boatmen enjoyed watching a personal encounter too much to join in. Gang warfare was not a habit among these ruffians.

The champion of a given crew, or set of crews—for vessels sometimes traveled in groups—proudly stuck a red feather in the band of his hat when he went ashore at Natchez, sometimes called Sodom-on-the-Gitche-Gumee, or when he arrived at Girod Street, New Orleans—a district known as "The Swamp" and never entered by the police in less than squad strength. When he saw another man with a red feather he promptly called him out to the middle of the floor, while bets were made.

There was an instrument known as the tiger's claw, a clump of exquisitely sharp brass hooks, quite capable, when handled right, of taking the skin off the whole side of a man's face. This does not seem to have been used often. Bare fists were preferred.

There were two kinds of fist fights.

In a stand-up the two simply pummeled each other, principally in the face, until one took a backward step, or, more often, collapsed.

The rough-and-tumble was more popular, being bloodier, more varied, and covering a greater space. In a rough-and-tumble, *anything* went. The fighters might roll on the floor. They might hit with elbows, shoulders, feet: a knee to the testicles, when it could be managed, was applauded. Butting was allowed, and gouging. Biting too was in order. The cheek, an ear—these were choice morsels. Best of all was the end of the nose. A Mississippi boatman who had lost the tip of his nose never tried to conceal this mutilation, and indeed he displayed it with pride, as a Heidelberg student might display a *schläger Schmiss* on his cheek, treating it with salt from time to time to make sure that it did not heal and become invisible.

Gouging was the best. Fights were held with no other purpose than to see an eye worked out, dangling hideously at the end of its red string. This would end the proceedings. To gouge a man's eye out it was necessary first to get him down, flat on the floor, and to be on top of him in such a way that he could not appreciably squirm. He had probably been beaten into a semi-comatose state, or he would be able to wriggle away or at least to keep jerking his head back and forth. You got a thumb—two, if possible—under one of his eyeballs. You pressed in hard, and then up, with a scooping motion. The thing should come out easily, making a "pop," the echoes of which no doubt would be drowned in the shouts of applause that greeted your feat. Since the shock of pain probably had caused the poor wretch to faint, it would be easy enough to dredge out his other eye as well, while he was unconscious; but this was not usually done, for it was deemed unsportsmanlike. One eye, after all, was enough to settle the bets.

When a horde of men like this descended unpent upon some river town the prostitutes, the gamblers, and the tavern proprietors greeted them with a grin; but nobody else did. It went all the way back to James Willing. Anybody who came out of the north was hateful, for that was a land of evil. A Kaintuck was a man to be avoided.

The river men themselves cared not a whit what nation owned journey's end, the Crescent City. To them it was the place where they got paid off, and got drunk, and saw some fights. Spanish? French? What was the difference? They were all foreigners.

That France really owned Louisiana and was letting Spain administer it temporarily was by this time common knowledge; but few cared. Business was booming.

Then Don Juan Ventura Morales, the intendant at New Orleans, set off a bomb. It was brief, despite its world-rattling importance. It read:

> As long as it was necessary to tolerate the trade of neutrals, which is now abolished, it would have been prejudicial to this country, that the Intendant complying with his duty should have prevented the deposit in this city of the property of Americans as granted to them by the twenty-second article of the Treaty of Friendship, Limits and Navigation of the 27th of October 1795, at the expiration of the three years prefixed; but now that, with the publication of the treaty of Amiens, and the re-establishment of the communication between the English and Spanish subjects, that inconvenience has ceased, considering that the 22nd article of the said treaty prevents my continuing this toleration, which necessity required after the fulfillment of the stipulated time, this ministry can no longer consent to it, without an express order of the King's. Therefore without prejudice to the exportation of what has been admitted in proper time, I order that from this date shall cease the privilege which the Americans had of bringing and depositing their goods in this capitol. And that the foregoing may be publicly known, and that nobody may plead ignorance, I order it to be published in the accustomed places, copies to be posted up in public; and that the necessary notice be given of it to the Department of Finance, Royal Custom-House, and others that may be thought proper.
>
> Done at the Intendancy, signed with my hand, and countersigned by the Notary Public of Finance, at New Orleans, 16th October, 1802.

The reaction was instantaneous, and it stung. The governor at New Orleans, Don Juan de Salcedo, promptly protested to Washington and to Madrid that Morales had acted irresponsibly and that he had no authority for what he did. This would make no difference to the Intendant, for the Purse was independent of the Sword, and just at that time the two were not speaking to each other anyway. The Spanish ambassador at Washington, the Marquis de Caso Yrujo, notified Secretary of State Madison that he thought Morales had made a tragic mistake and that he was telling Madrid so. Yrujo was married to an American girl, a daughter of the governor of Pennsylvania, who was a prominent republican, and he shuddered to think what the desperate Federalists would do with such an issue. The legislature of Kentucky objected vehemently, and Governor Garrard sent a copy of its resolution to the President, along with a letter of his own expressing fear of an outbreak that he might not be able to control.

Jefferson himself, who dreaded war, at first tried to tut-tut the matter. In his annual message to Congress for 1803 he did not even mention the sealing off of the Mississippi, saying only: "The cession of the Spanish province of Louisiana to France, which took place in the course of the late war, will, if carried into effect, make a change in the aspect of our foreign relations which will doubtless have a just weight in any deliberations of the Legislature connected with that subject."

The President had not received the enfevered Kentucky legislative response before he framed his message. He was soon to learn that the Marquis de Caso Yrujo was right in his prognostication. The Federalists, who had been nearing their last gasp, had a field day, lambasting the milk-and-water policies of a President who would endure in silence such an affront. The Federalists suddenly had become the defenders of the poor mistreated men of the west. They called for war against Spain, while Spain still was the only *official* proprietor of Louisiana, though they never said what they might do if France decided to stand by her Family Compact friend and get into the fight. Senator James Ross, of Pennsylvania, a Federalist, made it definite. He called upon Congress to put $5,000,000 into the hands of the President, who with this would raise 50,000 men and take New Orleans. The measure was debated for a long time, in secret sessions, in both houses; and it took all Thomas Jefferson's skill and stamina to cause it to be dropped.

Jefferson replied to Governor Garrard that he was appointing a special ambassador to the court at Paris, a man who would be authorized to purchase the city and island of New Orleans, which nestled against the *east* bank of the Mississippi, and if possible West Florida and even East Florida as well, spending for this up to the sum of 50,000,000 *livres tournois*, which would come to about $9,250,000. The least they should settle for, the President decreed, was a permanent reshipment depot on the lower Mississippi near New Orleans. He did not even mention the territory *west* of the big river, Louisiana proper.

Jefferson informed the Kentucky governor, and at the same time the Congress in Washington, that the ambassador he had picked for this purpose was James Monroe, a fellow Virginian who was known to be a sharp, hard-driving lawyer. It had all been a ghastly mistake, Jefferson admitted, but Mr. Monroe would set it to rights.

Monroe, who already had done more than his share of public service, as he saw it, and who was anxious to settle down to private practice and make a little money, was by no means eager to take the assignment. Jefferson talked him into it. "Some men are born for the public," Jefferson told him. Monroe was to get $9,000 a year and travel expenses. He sighed, and accepted the instructions, and sailed for France.

14

Big Deal

MR. LIVINGSTON WAS HARD of hearing. His companion, Charles Maurice de Talleyrand-Périgord, an *ancien régime* holdover, silky and silken, all iridescence, habitually spoke in a low tone; and now Mr. Livingston asked the man if he would mind saying that again.

Talleyrand complied. He waved a hand that was encrusted with gems.

"Why not buy the whole territory?" he asked.

That was what Mr. Livingston, a New York lawyer, diplomat, and Federalist, *thought* that the prince had said. It was incredible, yet there it was. Mr. Livingston too was a holdover, and he suspected that his diplomatic days in Paris would not last long. He knew, definitely, that the bright young Virginia republican, James Monroe, was on his way from the States not as a replacement but as a co-worker with equal powers to try to get France to sell New Orleans and West Florida, perhaps even East Florida as well. Monroe would arrive any day now. Meanwhile Livingston was doing whatever he could to squeeze some sort of promise out of the dainty, saturnine Talleyrand, for he knew that as soon as

ROBERT LIVINGSTON, AMERICAN AMBASSADOR TO FRANCE

Monroe got into the act he would claim—for himself and for his party—all the credit for whatever success there was. Hence, Mr. Livingston pressed.

He knew something else. He knew that Talleyrand would not even have mentioned the rest of Louisiana, that vast unknown territory west of the Mississippi, much less suggest that the United States try to buy it, unless he had been instructed to do so by the all-powerful First Consul. Napoleon Bonaparte never permitted his lieutenants any latitude. Theirs not to reason why, theirs not to make reply, theirs but to do or die.

Livingston leaned forward. He began excitedly to bargain. But one person cannot bargain alone. A bout of bargaining is like an argument: it takes two. Talleyrand, that coruscating, unpredictable aristocrat, changed the subject. Livingston in his excitement started to go on; but he checked himself. The more eager Livingston seemed, the cooler would the elegant Frenchman become. It was a rule of the game. Livingston pulled himself up short, and he too waved a careless hand. Oh, no, he said. He had no authority, even if he had been interested, to buy any property west of the Mississippi River. His orders were only to price New Orleans and the Floridas.

"Perhaps when your successor has come—"

Here was a trick Talleyrand had often applied of late. He knew of course that James Monroe was on his way, and he was wont to anger Livingston by starting to say, "After you have been superseded—" thus indicating that the present conversation was only exploratory, a preliminary talk-over, nothing that could be regarded as final. This time, however, the New York man having been dizzyingly made aware of the stakes involved, dropped the subject.

He returned to it, dutifully, the next day. Of course, he began, there would be no sense in talking terms about the purchase of Louisiana because his country could not even think of such a thing. The United States, Livingston said,

CHARLES MAURICE DE TALLEYRAND-PÉRIGORD, NAPOLEON
BONAPARTE'S MOUTHPIECE

already was too big. Big republics didn't work out well, as
everybody knew. Still, while they were here, and as long as
they had nothing else to do, could perhaps his highness explain how he offered for sale a territory that France had not
yet taken over and that in any event she was bound by the
retrocession treaty of October 1, 1800, a treaty negotiated by
General Berthier with Godoy, the Prince of Peace, never to
sell or otherwise dispose of?

(For the French had persisted in their efforts to get Louisiana back, and under the dynamic leadership of the First Consul they had managed it at last. Carlos IV's scruples about accepting Papal land had been overcome, and the promise of the Kingdom of Etruria for the Duke of Parma, who had married the Infanta, had been solemnly renewed, while Bonaparte vowed that once he got Louisiana back he would never let any other nation have it. Robert R. Livingston knew this. The treaty was supposed to be secret, but Livingston, who had his spies, knew about it and he had even seen a copy of it.)

Talleyrand negligently shook his head. No, there was no such treaty, he sighed. At one time there had been "some talk" about such a thing, but nothing more.

It was then that Livingston knew for certain that this perfumed popinjay had his orders from Bonaparte. He would not have taken the trouble to deny what he must have known Livingston knew to be true, had it been otherwise. Livingston, therefore, pushed the point. Talleyrand like a snake slithered away.

When Livingston thought it over, putting the pieces together, it became clear to him why Bonaparte wished to sell not just New Orleans but all Louisiana. The explanation lay across the sea.

France some time before had forced out of her sister Spain the eastern end of the West Indian island of Hispaniola or Santo Domingo. France already had held the western part of that island, known as Haiti. All the black slaves, the French-speaking ones, the Spanish-speaking ones, had risen in August of 1791, and, after a great deal of savage slaughter that reduced the whole island to a state of anarchy, they had driven virtually all the whites out, to become the first Negro republic. In 1794 the French National Assembly, a little late, had abolished slavery in Santo Domingo. However, when, at the end of the century, General Bonaparte came into power, all this was changed. There was none of that *Liberté-Egalité-Fraternité* nonsense about the First Consul. He soon notified the blacks of Haiti that all was off and they were back in bondage, and in case there should be any dispute about this, he hit them with what he usually used when he wanted to back up a command—an army.

It was a very good army too, composed largely of veterans, and under the command of Leclerc, who was perhaps the best general that Bonaparte had just then, and certainly was one of the most experienced, and who additionally was the First Consul's brother-in-law, having married Bonaparte's lovely and lecherous sister Pauline. This army was supposed only to pause at Haiti in order to stamp out the pestiferous insurrectionists, after which it would go on to New Orleans, where they would annex for France the whole Territory of Louisiana and perhaps those of West and East Florida as well.

The blacks of Haiti, however, weren't finished yet. Under the command of a genius named Toussaint l'Ouverture they kept on fighting. Between them and yellow fever the French lost seventeen thousand men, including fifteen generals, one of them Leclerc himself, in a few months, though this was only supposed to be a side-duty.

L'Ouverture—"this gilded African," Bonaparte called him —was tricked into giving himself up. He was made all sorts of promises, and asked to go to France and confer with the First Consul about a plan for full freedom for the people of Haiti. As soon as he emerged from the jungle he was clapped into irons and taken to France—but not to Bonaparte. He was thrown into the fortress of Joux in the Jura Mountains, a damp place, where he soon died of pleuropneumonia. The men of Haiti, however, fought on.

A second expedition, originally designed to go to New Orleans directly, was diverted as reinforcements to the island of Santo Domingo, where the same thing happened all over again—yellow fever, malaria, and assorted ailments combining with Toussaint's fellow countrymen under half a dozen

other leaders, equally savage if not equally talented, to cut
it to pieces. A third expedition, this one to be headed by
General Rochambeau, a son of the General Rochambeau
who did so much to help the Americans win at Yorktown,
was gathered—and then disbanded. Fifty thousand men, fifty
thousand of the best-trained and best-equipped soldiers in
the world, already had disappeared into Santo Domingo like
snow upon the desert's dusty face; and Bonaparte wanted no
more of it. He was not an upholder of lost causes. He never
believed in throwing good money after bad. He knew when
he was licked, and said so. That men might call him a
coward, a quitter, even a traitor, troubled him not one bit.
What he did was right, he knew, because *he* did it.

All this Robert Livingston knew, and when he studied
the facts for only a moment he saw why the First Consul was
not merely willing but eager to sell Louisiana. He could not
hope to keep that place, once he had taken it from Spain—
and *that* part would be easy enough—unless he had either a
larger navy than that of Great Britain or some manner of
way station between France and the mouth of the Mississippi. He had lost Santo Domingo, and there was no other
site immediately available. Even if he could spare the men—
and his enormous conscription armies gulped men by the
tens of thousands—he could not hope, in his lifetime, to out-
build the English at sea. Moreover, he was committed to an
invasion of England. The two countries were not yet at war,
but Bonaparte had virtually announced his intention of declaring that war as soon as he was ready, and meanwhile the
formation of the invasion army was going on openly. So he
would sell Louisiana. He could use the money to finish the
invasion preparations. Once he had overrun Great Britain,
something he never doubted his ability to do, there would be
time enough to take Louisiana back. There would be no
British navy then, and the new little republic, the United
States of America, could offer only a contemptible opposition.

April 10 of that momentous year 1803 was Easter Sunday. James Monroe had landed at Havre and was on his way up to Paris. The First Consul notified the Prince Talleyrand and François, Marquis de Barbé-Marbois, to meet him in his private chambers after the Easter services at St. Cloud. The prince was the foreign minister, the marquis the minister of finance. Each had spent about a year in the United States, Talleyrand as an exile, Barbé-Marbois as a secretary of legation, but there was this important difference between them: Barbé-Marbois liked the Americans, Talleyrand didn't. Now Napoleon Bonaparte told them to sell Louisiana, the first time anybody had heard of such a plan.

Talleyrand got his chance the very next morning, Monday, when Livingston by preappointment was pleading with him to sell New Orleans. It was then that the foreign minister had asked, so casually, why the United States did not buy the whole territory of Louisiana, thereby sending Robert Livingston into a temporary state of shock. Talleyrand would go no further.

The following day, Tuesday, Monroe arrived, still shaky from the trip, and went to his prepared quarters. A tall young man with understanding gray-blue eyes and a friendly outgoing manner, he was no stranger in Paris. He had served there as United States ambassador in 1794–96. Just now he was in poor health. Much of the time, even while the property transaction was under way, he remained flat on his back, missing, however, nothing.

Livingston gave a dinner for Monroe the following night, Wednesday, April 13, at his, Livingston's, quarters. After the meal, and after they had all retired to the withdrawing room, the host, happening to glance out of a window, saw the Marquis de Barbé-Marbois strolling through the garden. In what must be listed among the strangest coincidences in history the finance minister had "just happened" to be passing the United States embassy and had "just happened" to feel like a stroll through its grounds. Livingston called him in for a drink.

JAMES MONROE WAS COMMISSIONED TO PURCHASE THE CITY AND
ISLAND OF NEW ORLEANS.

Barbé-Marbois was apologetic and did not stay long, but
he did tell Livingston, in an undertone, about the instructions
the First Consul had given him and the foreign affairs minister the previous Sunday morning, and he proposed that if the
ambassador wished to learn more he might drop in on him,
Barbé-Marbois, some time around midnight.

Livingston went there as soon as he could get rid of his
guests, and Barbé-Marbois mentioned 125,000,000 francs,
quickly, however, coming down to 80,000,000. Yes, he meant
for the whole Louisiana territory, including the island and
city of New Orleans. But he would not talk about the

Floridas. Livingston promptly named a lesser sum, and they began to haggle.

Thus, in an atmosphere of hush-hush, as if they were so many thieves, was started the discussion that led to the biggest real estate deal in history.

There was a reason for the secrecy—besides, that is, the diplomats' instinctive belief that no official act should be acknowledged until hands had been shaken, vows made, and the agreement signed, sealed, and wrapped in ribbons.

The public in France at that time had very little to say, for it had almost no way of asserting itself. The days of screaming mobs, of sans-culottes, of public trials, were gone. They had existed only a few years back, to be sure, but it might as well have been centuries.

It is likely that most of the people of France would have objected to the sale of Louisiana, if only as a matter of pride. But who could be sure? And how, in any event, could most of the people of France make themselves heard?

There was still a legislature of two chambers, but the First Consul paid little attention to it. He never consulted anybody, but simply announced his decisions, which were final. Two of his brothers, Lucien and Joseph, called upon him one morning while he was yet in his bath, happily splashing scented water about, and tried to tell him that he should never, in any circumstances, sell Louisiana. He screamed back at them that he would do as he pleased. *L'état, c'était lui.* Joseph went so far as to swear that he would lead the opposition in the chambers, and Napoleon asked, What chambers? Scenes like this were common at the Tuileries, for the Bonapartes were a hysterical lot. This one, it seems, must have been especially strident, for the valet who was supposed to attend Napoleon out of the bath, a Swiss, fainted.

Meanwhile Monroe and Livingston were dickering with Barbé-Marbois and the Prince Talleyrand.

Nobody knew how big Louisiana was. It was certainly bounded on the east by the Mississippi, and on the south by

THE LOUISIANA PURCHASE TERRITORY—1803

The Louisiana Purchase Territory—1803

the Gulf of Mexico at least as far west as the Sabine River. North it was supposed to go to the source of the Mississippi, but where was the source of the Mississippi? On the west Louisiana was believed to be bounded by the Rocky Mountains, which had not been surveyed.

There was no discussion, then, about boundaries. Nor was there any talk of mines, quarries, or other amassments of material, which, as far as could be determined, did not exist in the territory.

No, the talk was entirely about price. The two Frenchmen knew that the Americans, in any case, were exceeding their authority. They had somewhat less than $10,000,000 to spend, and this would have been a ridiculously low price for New Orleans and all the rest of Louisiana.

It was agreed, at last, that the deal should be done in French francs, the more stable of the two currencies, and that the money should be transferred through certain Dutch banks, which were named.

But—how *much* money?

There was an additional complication. The American ambassadors had instructions to collect, if they could, on the many claims of American nationals against French privateers in the late undeclared war between the two nations. These should be paid, it was agreed, but how much did they amount to? Nobody was sure. And should these claims be paid as a lump sum determined in advance, or should they be a percentage of the total payment for Louisiana, and, if the latter, then what percentage?

Napoleon Bonaparte was not a long-suffering man. He knew well enough that the sale of Louisiana would be unpopular with his people, but, though he had the bayonets to ignore this, he still was likely to change his mind at any moment. When the dickering had been going on for two whole weeks he showed unmistakable signs of impatience. The bargainers on both sides redoubled their efforts.

The Americans proposed a total of 70,000,000 francs, of

which 50,000,000 should be paid direct and the remainder paid by the United States government to its own nationals who had valid claims against the French. Marbois and Talleyrand whispered fearfully that the First Consul never would accept such a price. The very least he would accept, they were sure, they said, was 80,000,000 francs, of which 60,000,-000 would be in cash. And it was upon this figure that the four agreed, May 2.

They shook hands all around, congratulating one another, and Livingston and Monroe sat down to write a long letter of explanation to the American secretary of state.

Napoleon Bonaparte, perhaps with an eye on public opinion after all, meaning to soften the blow a little, announced that the money would all be spent for canals. Canals would be dug back and forth throughout the country.

His real reason for forcing the deal through [34] he freely admitted to those around him: "I have given England a rival who sooner or later will humble her pride."

That price of 80,000,000 francs came to about $15,000,-000. The territory to change hands, though its exact limits had not been established, was known to be almost four times as large as the thirteen original colonies, more than seven times as large as Great Britain and Ireland put together, and about three times as big as Italy. Calling it one million square miles, which was as good a guess as any, the United States had paid about four cents a square mile for it.

15

Anybody But a Politician

THE NEWS REACHED AMERICA June 30, and the splash that it made was stupendous, the ripples high and hissing. France had reacted as loudly as France dared, but this was as nothing to the yelp of astonishment that rose from the United States, which awoke one morning to find itself a major power, doubled in size.[35]

Westerners, as soon as they had finished gasping, cheered the deed. Anything that assured an open river they favored. No price would have been too high to pay for that. Of the eastern states, residents, southerners in general approved the Purchase, though they were a bit bewildered; middle staters had reservations, at least at first; and the New Englanders, the last of the Federalists, were bitterly opposed.

The too-big prophets were horrified. They had long been awaiting the dissolution of the Union, which, they thought, was unwieldy; but now there was no hope for it, and it would disintegrate, or explode.

The notion was not a new one. For centuries political thinkers had conceded that the republican form of government would be all right *if* it was kept within reasonable bounds, the bounds being, it would seem, about the size of your Aunt Ellen's backyard. A large republic, these men contended, was a contradiction in terms. A classical example always was a clincher, and the man who listened was invited to look at ancient Rome. So long as Rome was a mere city-state it remained a republic, and a successful one; but as soon as it began to take on colonies it began also to take on Caesars, and the republic existed no longer. More recently there was Venice, and there was Switzerland, a nation with a great deal of geography but happily little history. Also, there was the Netherlands. In each of these republics, however, it should be noted that everybody who was anybody knew everybody else. They worked well because of their very tininess. Blown up in size, they would fall apart. Bigness would be a blight for them.

That the American colonies habitually snarled at and cursed one another was no secret to European observers. Only the crown, monarchy, the "natural" way of governing, it was cheerfully predicated, had kept them together this long. Released from its beneficent pressure the states would simply fly off into nothingness.

It was not only the crowlike croakers along the battlements who believed this. It was, as well, the sober citizens who approved of and applauded the Great Experiment. These too shook sad heads. They feared that the Purchase would be a backward step in the fight for freedom.

Most of the citizens, however, seemed to find it exhilarating to be suddenly so rich—rich, that is, in land.

There were those who believed that the opening of the vast plains country to Americans might result in a second nation, a rival to the west. The Spaniards had done virtually nothing about the Louisiana Territory, so there were no precedents. Lewis and Clark, though they had been commissioned to make their historic exploration before the Louisiana Purchase had been thought of, had not yet started forth into what until just now was Spanish territory. Daniel Boone might carry on with his rifle and his traps along the banks of the Great Muddy, but Boone was a loner and no answer to any colonization problem. For a long time the drillmaster of Valley Forge, the Baron von Steuben, had been trying to get Spanish permission to establish a 200,000-acre settlement along the west bank of the Mississippi more or less opposite the mouth of the Ohio, and he had stressed that this would be a strictly non-military venture, an agricultural venture; but he never did receive an answer from Madrid.

Nobody, it should be noted, had put his finger upon the real danger involved in the acquisition of Louisiana. Nobody at that time was able to foresee that cotton would become king in the south; that slavery, cooped up, could not survive, and would start to slop over into the west, a movement that was to bring about the greatest of all civil wars. Slavery in 1803 was an archaic and rather disgusting institution, a malodorous institution; but it did not loom as a menace.

The political implications were the most puzzling part of the Monroe-Livingston triumph. The Federalists of course were against the Purchase; and the Federalists were desperate men, concerned with keeping themselves alive. Just as the morose Mr. Livingston had predicted when he learned that Mr. Monroe was crossing the sea in order to assist him, the republicans took all the credit. The deal had been made by a republican ambassador serving under a republican President and a republican secretary of state. Therefore the Federalists were opposed to it.

One might suppose that the Federalists would applaud an act that seemed to grant the executive department all but unlimited power, since their whole *raison d'être* was belief in central authority, just as the republicans existed only because they believed in a weak President and scattered power. This was not to be. Each of the two parties, without a blush, reversed itself. It was the first time that this had happened in the history of the United States, but it was not to be the last. Anybody but a politician would have been embarrassed.

Thomas Jefferson *was* embarrassed, and showed it. For years he had been insisting upon the "strict construction" theory, saying again and again that the only powers Congress had were those specifically delegated to it by the Constitution and those necessary to carry the delegated powers into effect. This was, in his own words, "the very breath of my political life."

He summoned Congress to a special session.

There was one objection to the Purchase that worried Jefferson not at all. This was the price. He himself, like almost everybody else even remotely connected with the deal, thought that $15,000,000 was dirt cheap; yet there were newspapers, Federalist of course, that tried to make it seem extravagant. Manhattan Island, they pointed out with a perfectly straight face, had been bought for trade goods worth about $24; Sir Ferdinando Gorges had been sold Maine for £1,250, and William Penn had paid only a little over £5,000 for all of Pennsylvania. The price it was proposed to pay for Louisiana, these minority journals squealed, would make up 433 *tons* of pure silver, which would fill 866 wagons, making a procession 5⅓ miles long. In the form of silver dollars, piled up on one another, this would reach three miles into the air. The sum of $15,000,000, these papers went on, would pay for an army of 25,000 men (the United States Army *had* numbered 5,000 men, but lately, on coming into office, Jefferson had reduced it to 3,000) at $8 a week for 25 years. Why, just the interest on that sum would support forever 1,800 free schools, allowing $500 a year a school, which would accommodate 90,000 pupils. Did you realize that $15,000,000, which those crazy men in Washington are talking of paying for a vast wasteland nobody knows anything about, represents $3 for every man, woman, and child in the whole country?

These trivia did not trouble the serene-seeming Jefferson. He was concerned first with the question of whether the

United States *could* buy Louisiana, and, secondly, with what should be done with it after it *had* been bought. He worried in particular about the rights of the Indians there. Nobody even knew how many there were.

As he saw it, the Constitution would not permit the purchase of foreign territory, even contiguous territory, since it said nothing about that. He had no faith in the so-called *implied* powers the Federalists talked about. Therefore, the Constitution must be amended before the Purchase could be put through; and already Livingston and Monroe were writing from Paris to beg him to move fast, for the First Consul might change his mind at any moment.

Jefferson even framed an amendment he meant to submit to Congress and the state legislatures. In fact, he framed two of them. The first started bravely enough: "The province of Louisiana is incorporated with the United States and made part thereof," but soon degenerated into an uncharacteristic windiness, suggesting that the President was unsure of himself, as the friends he showed it to admitted. Then he framed a much shorter one, but the same friends found this too "scared" a statement, and he scrapped it.

John Quincy Adams, a painfully conscientious man, confided to his diary at this time that he could not sleep because of worrying about the Louisiana proposition. He too framed a constitutional amendment, but *none* of *his* friends liked it, and it was allowed to drop.

The secretary of state, little James Madison, proposed the simplest, clearest amendment of them all. It consisted of "Louisiana is hereby admitted to this Union." Nobody paid any attention to it.

Though there were many friends who urged upon President Jefferson that the treaty-making power conferred by the Constitution would cover the Louisiana Purchase, making an amendment unnecessary, Wilson Cary Nicholas is generally credited with being the one who convinced him of this. The

President's first reaction was: "If the treaty-making power is boundless, then we have no Constitution." But at last he gave in. The bargain was too tempting.

The only person who spoke up for Spain, poor Spain, was the Marquis de Caso Yrujo. For all his sympathy with the Jefferson administration, he felt called upon to remind Secretary of State Madison that the Louisiana Purchase would not be legal, since Napoleon Bonaparte had never owned what he purported to sell. Bonaparte, Yrujo averred, had solemnly promised to set up the kingdom of Etruria, yet it was French generals who in fact continued to rule those Tuscan provinces. The French government had made much of the young Duke of Parma and his wife, the Spanish Infanta, staging costly fêtes in their honor, heaping them with decorations, "majestying" them diligently; but where was that throne? The "king" had recently died—May 27—having been acknowledged by no other nation than France itself; and did anyone believe that his widow and his son ever would rule over Etruria, as Bonaparte had promised? Moreover, there was the indisputable fact that Bonaparte had sworn never to cede or to sell Louisiana. Godoy, the Prince of Peace, had insisted upon this. Bonaparte hated the prince—*"ce misérable"*—the only man in Europe who would stand up to him—but he had complied.

This was Spain's complaint; but it was not the fashion to listen to Spain.

More serious were the objections raised by the strict constructionists, who were now, of course, the Federalists. Section 3 of Article IV of the United States Constitution, these statesmen pointed out, read:

> New States may be admitted by the Congress into this Union; but no new State shall be formed or erected within the jurisdiction of any other State, nor any State be formed by the junction of two or more States or parts

of States, without the consent of the Legislatures of the States concerned, as well as of the Congress.

The Congress shall have power to dispose of and make all needful rules and regulations respecting the territory or other property belonging to the United States; and nothing in this Constitution shall be so construed as to prejudice any claims of the United States, or of any particular State.

This meant, the Federalists triumphantly cried, that *all of the states*, besides Congress, would have to ratify the Purchase treaty; and nobody pretended that such a thing was possible as long as the Federalists kept their grip on New England.

What's more, the Federalists went on, the seventh article of the proposed treaty, the Purchase treaty, read:

That the French ships coming directly from France or any of her colonies, loaded only with the produce and manufactures of France or her said colonies; and the ships of Spain coming directly from Spain or any of her colonies, loaded only with the produce or manufactures of Spain or her colonies, shall be admitted during the space of twelve years in the port of New Orleans, and in all other legal ports of entry within the ceded territory, in the same manner as the ships of the United States coming directly from France or Spain, or any of their colonies, without being subject to any other or greater duty on merchandise, or other or greater tonnage than that paid by the citizens of the United States.

How, the Federalists demanded, did the Jeffersonians reconcile that with Article I, Section 9 of the Constitution, which stipulates that "No preference shall be given by any regulation of commerce or revenue to the ports of one State over those of another"?

Congress met, though it took more than a week to get a quorum.

The Senate inside of four days voted 24 to 7 for ratification of the Purchase treaty. Spain's complaint was ignored. The Federalist contention that all of the states would have to ratify such a treaty was considered, but not seriously and not for long. The contention that the "free port" clause of the treaty would clash with Article I, Section 9, was met and pulverized by a triumph of the legal mind: The constitutional clause only related to commerce between the several states, whereas the treaty clause concerned commerce between the states on one side and a territory on the other; hence there was no clash.

The House was not so easily handled. It had no business here; but, as it had done in the case of the ratification of the Jay treaty in 1796, it pushed its way into the debate. Gaylord Griswold, a representative from New York, and a Federalist, introduced into the House a resolution calling for a better look at the French claim to Louisiana. *Did* France in fact have the right to sell the place? The vote was very close— 59 to 57—but Griswold's resolution lost. This was the nearest its enemies ever came to blocking the Louisiana Purchase.

Of the twenty-five who voted against ratification in both houses seventeen were New Englanders, and all were Federalists.[36]

On the last day of November in a pouring rain before the Cabildo in New Orleans the Spanish flag was run down, the French flag was run up. In the same square, the Place d'Armes,[37] December 20, the French flag was run down, the Stars and Stripes raised, and the territory of Louisiana was accepted in the name of the United States—in English, since neither of them could speak a word of Spanish or French— by the new governor, William Charles Coles Claiborne, and

On December 20, 1903, the French flag was run down the pole before the Cabildo in New Orleans, and the Stars and Stripes was raised.

the commander-in-chief of the United States Army, James Wilkinson. It was a clear day, sunny and bright.

The money was paid, on time. But it did not go toward the digging of canals. It all went into the army for invasion of England, an invasion that never took place.

CHAPTER

16

Go West, Middle-aged Man

THOUGH IT LOOKED LIKE a good July day, clear and warm, Mr. Van Ness carried an umbrella when he went to the dueling ground. He and Colonel Burr got there first, but General Hamilton and Mr. Pendleton came soon afterward in another boat. Dr. Hosack was left with the boatmen down by the edge of the river, at a spot hidden from the field by bushes.

They fired. Hamilton's ball clipped the branch of a cedar about 12½ feet up, some 13 or 14 feet from where the duelist stood, and about 4 feet from the line of fire. Burr's ball smashed Hamilton's second or third false rib and then passed through his liver and diaphragm to lodge in one of the lower vertebrae.

Hamilton fell forward and a little to the left—that is, away from the cedar tree. Mr. Pendleton rushed to his side. Colonel Burr, smoking pistol in hand, started toward him, as though to offer condolences, but such an offer would have been highly irregular, and Mr. Van Ness went swiftly to him and led him off, down the path to the shore. The boatmen and Dr. Hosack had heard the shots, and they were scram-

151

bling up the slope. When he and his principal passed them Mr. Van Ness was holding the opened umbrella before Colonel Burr's face, so that none of them could swear, afterward, that he had actually seen the colonel coming away from the field. It was for this purpose that Mr. Van Ness had brought the umbrella.

He might have saved himself the trouble. The biggest shade in the world could not have concealed Aaron Burr's face from a shocked world. Anyway, he never meant to hide.

There had been duels before; there would be duels again, and many of them; but there never before had been such a flare-up of fury against the system that made them possible. It was like the explosion of a bomb.

Here were two heroes of the Revolution. One was Vice-President of the United States, the other until recently had been secretary of the treasury, the nation's first, and for a little while secretary of war. Yet at the time they fought they were political bankrupts. Hamilton, an arrogant little bastard —he stood 5 feet 7 inches—never had held elective office, and owed his position in the cabinet as well as his position in the army almost entirely to the faith George Washington, now dead, had had in him. He considered the public a "great beast," and believed that the Constitution was weak and would soon fall apart. Burr, personally lovable, was a loner, a reserved man who seemed always to be holding something back. People enjoyed his company, but few leaned upon him, for he was thought to be unreliable. The breath of scandal never had grazed him, yet somehow he had the air of an adventurer, a man who'd try anything, a desperate man. His own political superior, Thomas Jefferson, now the President, did not trust him. Nobody could explain this. It was a feeling, an inner conviction, rather than a reasoned belief.

Now, abruptly, Alexander Hamilton had become a saint, a martyr, while Aaron Burr was an unspeakable fiend.

When Hamilton died, the day after the duel, having suffered hideously in the meanwhile, New England and the

Middle Atlantic states flew into a rage. In the South and the West, where such meetings were more common—though they were by no means *unknown* in the North—there seemed no reason to gnash the teeth or beat the breast. Burr had behaved properly, hadn't he? In fact, when the evidence was all examined it became apparent that he had behaved extremely well—better, probably, than Alexander Hamilton deserved.

Burr, for all his reserve, was a friendly man. He liked people. Nobody had ever heard him say anything harsh about anybody else. Hamilton, who had a short temper, was not that way. When there was something that he didn't like he said so, and he said so about Aaron Burr again and again, though never in public and never in writing. Hamilton felt very strongly about this. He believed that Burr would be bad for the country, and he told his friends so in the privacy of their homes. Burr heard; but for a long time there was nothing that he could do.

The two had met often in the courtroom and at formal dinners. Once they had met in connection with an *incipient* duel. Burr liked women, yet while she lived he was faithful to his wife, the widow of a British army colonel, with five children, whom Burr had married when he was twenty-six. After her death—well, that was another story. Many bastards were attributed to Colonel Burr, who, however, never tattled. With Alexander Hamilton it was different. Hamilton had married, very young, into the powerful and wealthy Schuyler family, and had fathered eight children. He was for a long time systematically unfaithful to the former Elizabeth Schuyler, his companion in this romp being a certain Mrs. Reynolds of New York. Hamilton supposed the lady to be a widow, at first; but soon a husband appeared, and the process of blackmail set in. Then suddenly the whole affair was made public. Hamilton, furious, blamed the publicity on James Monroe of Virginia. Monroe was utterly innocent of this, and so stated; but Hamilton continued to call him angry names, and Monroe thought that he should challenge. Monroe, then, called in his friend Colonel Burr, whom he asked to carry a challenge to Alexander Hamilton. Hamilton had expected him, but Burr was startled to learn that the secretary of the treasury thought that he carried not a challenge but an offer to apologize. This caused both principals to be embarrassed; but Burr, equal to the occasion, and as affable a man as ever lived, talked Hamilton out of his pet and got him to agree to sign a statement—written on the spot by Colonel Burr himself—that made everybody feel better all around; and there was no fight.

Now, in the late spring of 1804, there fell into Burr's hands a clipping from an upstate paper that quoted an obscure clergyman as saying that Alexander Hamilton had stigmatized Colonel Burr as a man not to be trusted. There was more; but this was the tenor of the thing. Burr sent the clipping to Hamilton. He did not demand an apology, only asked for an explanation. The note was a mite stiff—some stiffness in the circumstances was only to be expected—but it was not rude.

Hamilton, though he certainly knew what was coming, pretended that he did not understand what Burr wanted. He named a friend, as Burr had done, and for nine days these friends went back and forth with messages. Burr's notes were short, and he stuck to the point. Hamilton, ordinarily a fine writer, rambled. He was querulous, and sometimes even blustered a bit. This was not like him. He could have been ill. It was disclosed, afterward, when Dr. Hosack handed the estate a bill for $37.50, that he had been treating Hamilton for some weeks for an alimentary complaint. (Dr. Hosack also turned in a bill for $50 for services in treating the gunshot wound suffered in Weehawken; and he collected on both of these.)

The first note was carried June 18, 1804, but not until June 27 was it definitely determined that there should be a confrontation. Even then Hamilton asked and was accorded another two weeks in which to clear up some court cases and also some personal affairs. He had got rid of Mrs. Reynolds some time earlier, but for a man who has been hailed in history as a financial genius he left his own money affairs in a muddle. Though he had been successful in private law practice, he was deeply in debt. He explained this in memorandum after memorandum, and also in notes to his second and to his executors-to-be. He was apologetic about it, which, once again, was not like him.

After Hamilton's death, the cry for vengeance was so loud, in the eastern states, that it seems almost certain that it must have had some outside assistance; but it is hard to see *what*. Neither Federalists nor republicans any longer wanted either man. They were a couple of burnt-out Roman candles.

Burr was to be accused of having rushed Hamilton into the business, which was certainly not so. Hamilton had protested in the various papers that he left that he was opposed to the practice of dueling; but if this was true, he chose a curious way to show his opposition. "Posting"—that is, publicly calling a man who refused to accept your challenge a craven coward and perhaps worse—had not yet been invented; it was to be America's one original contribution to the code duello; and no pressure was brought against Hamilton. He could have refused to fight. The affair was not advertised, and indeed it was one of the most discreetly arranged on record, for even the close friends of the two men had not suspected that there was trouble in the air.

Burr was depicted as an expert shot who had lured the innocent Hamilton to his undoing. Nonsense. Both men were veterans, though Hamilton's army experience was rather longer and fuller than Burr's. Each was represented by a respectable lawyer-and-friend, a man who knew what he was doing and why. They were both in their middle forties, Hamilton being by a year the younger. Both were short, Hamilton by one inch the taller. The surgeon in attendance was Hamilton's personal physician. On the field there were two coin tosses—for position and for calling the signal—and Hamilton, as it happened, won both.

The pistols probably were strange to both men, but if either had handled them previously it would have been Hamilton, for they belonged to his brother-in-law, John Barker Church.

Hamilton in his notes to his second had made much of his intention of firing into the air, at least for the first shot. Perhaps he did this. We will never know. It was Pendleton's belief that Burr had fired first, and that Hamilton had fired unwittingly under the shock of getting hit. It was Van Ness's opinion that Hamilton had fired first by a split second.

Burr was pictured, a Mephistophelian leer on his face, practicing with a pistol for weeks in advance. He was called a crack shot, an experienced duelist. Yet he had only once before been a principal in an affair of honor, and then he had missed.

This did not matter. The public needed a goat, and the public was in full bay.

A coroner's jury in New York, which had no right to do so, found "that Aaron Burr, late of the Eighth Ward of the said City in the said County Esquire and Vice President of the United States, not having the fear of God before his eyes, but being moved and seduced by the Instigation of the Devil, on the eleventh day of July in the year last aforesaid, with force and Arms, in the County of Bergen [38] and State of New Jersey in and upon the Said Alexander Hamilton in the peace of God and of the people, of the Said State of New Jersey, then and there being, feloniously Wilfully and of his Malice aforethought, did make and Assault, and that the Said Aaron Burr . . ." There was much, much more.[39]

Burr was a man who did not like crowds. He slipped away to New Jersey, and when a grand jury there indicted him for murder he went on to South Carolina to visit his daughter and son-in-law. He returned to the raw-new city of

AARON BURR

Washington when it was time for Congress to sit again, and he presided over the United States Senate as before, the very soul of dignity and impartiality. Nobody *there* called him nasty names.

Warrants for his arrest still stood in New Jersey and New York, and it was unlikely that these would be quashed, for his enemies, in New York in particular, did not want him back. Just before the duel he had perhaps been flirting with the Federalists of New England—it is not certain, for he was reticent about these matters—and it had seemed possible that he might jump to their side and head a secession government composed of New England, New York, and perhaps New Jersey. But this was no longer to be thought of, for the rickety Federalist party had made a martyr out of Alexander Hamilton. In New York the Livingstons and the Clintons long had had their knives bared for Aaron Burr, and their power was greater than ever, and growing. DeWitt Clinton, who was governor now, keeping the office in the family—his uncle had served four terms there—was especially vociferous in his denunciation of the "cold-blooded murderer," Aaron Burr. Clinton himself had fought a duel only a little earlier, firing no fewer than five times, twice winging his enemy in the thigh; but he preferred to forget this. Clinton was lucky that *he* had not been called out, instead of Hamilton. He had been every bit as scurrilous, and as careless, in his excoriation of Burr. He had long thirsted for Burr's power; and now indeed his Uncle George, the four-time governor, was to succeed Aaron Burr as Vice-President of the United States at the end of Jefferson's first term, for the President believed that he needed the help of the Clinton-Livingston machine.

Aaron Burr, then, had only two roads to march, for he couldn't stay home. He could go to Europe, or he could go west into the new country. He had a living to make. He went west.

He took his time about it, stopping often to visit old acquaintances, senators and the like, and being made much of. In Cincinnati he dallied for a long time with General Wilkinson, who was about to move his headquarters to the village of St. Louis; and it is a safe assumption that they discussed the Spanish Conspiracy, which was still alive. At Nashville he was entertained by Andrew Jackson, one of his most ardent admirers. In short, he saw everybody worth seeing. He was cheered and fawned upon. The West had never before seen such a man, and was flattered by a visit from the Vice-President—Burr still was Vice-President. He made speeches, necessarily; but he never said anything; he never gave a clue as to why he was there, or what if anything he sought.

All that had gone before was as nothing compared with the jubilation with which he was greeted in New Orleans. Here was no grizzled, frayed, blasphemous Kaintuck, but rather an urbane, dapper, French-speaking man of the world, one who had killed his traducer on the field of honor. New Orleans was predominantly French, and the creoles, hating the uncouth Yankees, hated and feared even more the Spaniards, whose nearest border, Texas, was uncomfortably close.

New Orleans knew how a football feels. When the Louisiana Purchase had been made known it was assumed by most of America that this would prove to be the final flipflop, that thereafter the Crescent City would remain tranquil and prosperous under one boss. Creoles did not think this. They had not been lifted into the shining realm of liberty, as other Americans seemed to suppose, for the ordinance under which they operated in the first days of United States sovereignty gave them in fact even less freedom and self-rule than they had known under either the Spaniards or the French. Understandably, they did not like this. They were ripe for revolt.

The Purchase did not precipitate a rush of Yankees to Louisiana, as might have been expected. River traffic increased, so that at any given time the city was filled with brawling, boisterous keelboatmen and flatboatmen; but the regular population of about nine thousand when Aaron Burr visited the city in the summer of 1805 remained unchanged. The few Yankee newcomers were merchants or lawyers, and were mostly successful, which did not endear them to the "ancient Louisianians." Such easterners as there were were not notable for their loyalty to the government on the other side of the mountains. Without being out-and-out treasonous, they inclined to the belief that a western government, independent of Washington, would be a good thing, and most vehemently did they agree with the "ancient Louisianians" that Mexico should be taken over before the dons there—Spaniards as distinct from Mexicans always were called "dons"—could snap up the Crescent City. These American newcomers, some three hundred in number—though the exact figures never will be known—had organized what they called the Mexican Association, a secret body the members of which were pledged to obtain any military information about Mexico that they could get by any means—agents in Mexico, correspondents, anything. This was clearly looking toward an invasion; and the Mexican Association naturally welcomed Aaron Burr, who looked like an answer to their prayers.

Daniel Clark, who, though of Welsh rather than Irish extraction, might be termed the mercantile successor to Oliver Pollock, did not belong to the Mexican Association. At least, he said that he did not, perhaps only for business reasons. He undoubtedly sympathized with their cause. Burr had brought a letter of introduction to Daniel Clark from General Wilkinson, and Burr and Clark were often seen together.

If all this talk about creating an empire would seem to be glittering dream-stuff and hardly the sort of thing that a businessman like Daniel Clark would for a moment consider, it should be remembered that the world was changing. There was already an Emperor of Brazil, a Portuguese. Only a few days earlier (on May 18, 1804), a penniless little Italian had made himself Emperor of France and had gone on to make one brother King of Holland, another King of Westphalia, and a third King of Spain. He scolded monarchs as though they were schoolboys and made them stand in corners. Why it should be remembered that the world was changing. There have been made for that purpose. And Aaron Burr, don't forget it, might have been made to be the emperor.

He loved New Orleans, which loved him. No matter what territorial complex might at last emerge from his intricate plottings, he told his daughter Theodosia in a letter that *this* would be his capital.

He stayed there for three weeks, and then, fairly bubbling with joyous memories, he took the river road up to Natchez for another round of banquets and conferences. After that he struck out for Nashville.

17

The Perilous Path

N ATCHEZ, at least that part of the town below the bluff, at the very river's edge, Natchez-under-the-Hill, was a congeries of brothels and bars and gambling houses, a putrescent stretch of sin, where no man was safe after dark. Aaron Burr, who had no fondness for low life, did not descend to this hell, but spent the days of his visit more profitably among the Bingmans, Surgets, Minors, Burneys, and Duncans, people who lived on the top of the bluff, and ate and drank well, and owned the Pharsalia race course, and from time to time blasted one another to death in accordance with carefully laid-down rules and with the greatest imaginable elegance.

After that, however, and attended by only a single servant (it was probably Peter, his favorite, a Negro), Burr rode forth upon the Natchez Trace.

It was called the most perilous thoroughfare in the world. A patch-together of old Indian trails, it reached 501 miles between Natchez and Nashville. Some of it was almost imperceptible. All of it was wild. It was Cherokee and Creek country, but the Creeks and Cherokee seldom annoyed travelers, for they only asked to be let alone. Instead, it was land pirates, white men, most of them fugitives from justice, who gave the Trace its bad name.

Flatboatmen and keelboatmen, having floated down the river to New Orleans and disposed of their wares, could sometimes sign on a vessel that was about to make the return trip—it took at least twice as many men to get a boat *up*-stream as it had taken to get it down—but the work was back-breaking, the wages were low, and it took a long time. Most of the boatmen, with money burning holes in their pockets, if they had not fallen prey to the harpies and the imperturbable faro dealers of New Orleans, preferred to go back by the route Aaron Burr took—the river road to Natchez, after that the Trace. Customarily they traveled in parties, but they were unused to the forest, so that they made easy marks for the land-pirates, who sometimes left them their underwear but sometimes killed them, disposing of the bodies by slicing these open and filling them with rocks and sinking them in some convenient stream or swamp.

Few of these ruffians lasted long enough at their chosen profession to accumulate even a modicum of notoriety. It was a short life, and anything but a merry one. James Mason was an exception. Tall, middle-aged, serious, he was a handsome man, or would have been considered such except for one long tooth that protruded fanglike from his upper jaw. He kept his wife with him. Her name was Marguerite; she had been Marguerite Douglas. Once Mason and one of his sons, captured in Natchez and found to be in possession of stolen goods, were each given a "Moses' dose" (thirty-nine lashes) and made to stand for twelve hours in the town pillory, but nobody knew that this was *the* James Mason, and he and his son were released.

Necessarily they moved about a good bit. From time to time they would cross the river into what was still Spanish territory, and it was in such a place that they were at last rounded up—Mason himself, his wife, his three sons, his daughter-in-law, three grandchildren, and two strangers, one named Taylor or Setton or Sutton, the other named Mays, not to mention some bolted silk, muslin, and cotton, miscellaneous coins, seven thousand dollars in United States paper money, many guns, a field stove, and camping gear. They were being sent down the river to New Orleans to stand trial when they escaped in a storm, scattering.

Soon afterward Sutton and Mays appeared in Natchez with a severed head preserved in blue clay, which they swore was that of James Mason. They were after the reward, of course; but they were not believed, and they were tried and found guilty, and hanged in a field outside Greenville, about twenty miles north of Natchez, on February 8, 1804, just a little before Aaron Burr's visit to those parts.

Mason had always said that he did not enjoy killing and would shoot a man only if that man offered resistance. It was not so with the brothers Harpe, about as mean a pair of cutthroats as the land ever had known.

Here was brutality epitomized. The Harpes had no apparent purpose in life; they pursued no career, practiced no art, carried out no plan, and did not make money. They robbed, but only on the side. They killed, however, senselessly, steadily. Killing was their life.

Micajah was by two years the older, and was always called "Big Harpe." He was, indeed, enormous. Black-haired, shaggy, scowling, he made such a frightful appearance that even sturdy frontiersmen froze at the sight of him. His brother Wiley, "Little Harpe," was of ordinary height and build, though he seemed small by the side of Micajah. He was red-headed.

What these monsters had against the world we never will know. Their violence was without direction. Had there been any sort of government in those parts—they wandered, more or less, the whole length of Tennessee and Kentucky, leaving bloody corpses and burned-down shacks behind them —they would have been captured early, for they never tried to cover their tracks, and they were encumbered by women.

There was a practice along the frontier known as "Bible marriage," whereby a couple in the absence of any preacher could lay their hands upon a copy of the Good Book and vow that they would be true to each other. Such a union usually was made legitimate when at last a circuit rider *did* appear, often a year or more later. There is no evidence that either of the Harpe brothers ever had taken part in even a Bible marriage. They simply brought their women with them.

Big Harpe had two, Susan and Betsey Roberts, who were sisters. Little Harpe's light-o'-love, one Sally Rice, was said to have been the daughter of a preacher. This *ménage à cinq* was broken up once, and the women were confined to a log cabin that served as a temporary jail while their lovers were being sought elsewhere. There, within the space of a month, Sally and Susan and Betsey produced three babies, one each. Two of these babies belonged to Big Harpe, or so the women said, and one was Little Harpe's.

When the women at last were released, after it had come to be believed that the Harpes were far away and would never return, they were released with prayers and with a certain amount of cash—rare in those parts, raised by neighbors who believed that these fallen sisters, these soiled doves, had been forced into a life of sin, and would, given a chance, go straight. The women instead promptly returned to the Harpes, whom they met at a predetermined point in the wilderness, and to whom they turned over the money.

The babies might have slowed the band down. One of them so annoyed Big Harpe by its bawling—it was one of his own, too—that he snatched it from its mother's arms and, holding it by the heels, smashed its head against a tree, killing it.

The Harpes created a region of terror out in that wild country, where men were reluctant to take part in posses for very long because they were afraid to leave their wives and children unprotected. Nevertheless, the Harpes were at last driven apart, and a small band of settlers went hell-bent for Micajah, Big Harpe. When they caught him there was no trumpery-flummery about arrest and confinement and law courts. They simply cut him to bits on the spot. They hacked off his head, for one thing, and hung it in a tree. This was in Webster County, Kentucky, far from the Natchez Trace that had been the Harpes' usual hunting ground; and the skull remained there for many years, a landmark. There is still a Harpe's Head Road in Webster County.

Little Harpe then disappeared, and the general belief for some time was that he had lost himself in the vast country west of the Mississippi, the illimitable Louisiana; yet when Mays and the robber called Sutton or Setton tried in vain to collect the reward for the death of James Mason, being hanged for their pains near Greenville, Mississippi, there were many to vow, afterward, that he had been in fact the late Wiley ("Little") Harpe. It could be true.

The women, relieved of these enormities, had no trouble getting legitimate husbands and settling down to normal backwoods life. Women were always in demand along the frontier, where men were willing to let bygones be bygones.

Aaron Burr, however, and Peter—if it was Peter—rode the whole length of this perilous path without seeing a single desperado. They were, perhaps, just lucky.

In Nashville Burr again was entertained by Andrew Jackson, who lent him a barge in which to drift down the Cumberland to the Ohio, where another and larger boat picked up Burr and his servant for the trip to St. Louis. Here again was a trip fraught with danger. The banks of the lower Ohio sheltered many a band of wreckers who would attack boats that were tied up for the night, and strip them, or sink them, or both. These rascals were especially thick around the mouth of the Cash River near Fort Massac, though one of the most famous of them, Colonel Fluger, originally of New Hampshire, and his fat wife Pluggy, preferred to operate a little lower down. Then too there was the notorious Cave in Rock to be passed. This place swarmed with river pirates. It was said that at one time even the far-ranging Harpe brothers had paid a visit there, but the regular residents, who, like James Mason, would shoot a man only when he resisted, and never just for the fun of the thing, found the Harpes too bloodthirsty for their somewhat simple tastes, and asked them to move on. Cave in Rock is twenty miles below Shawneetown, Illinois, and it is 165 feet long, 40 feet above low water, and 55 feet wide. Because of its peculiar location it was an ideal place from which to spot craft coming down the river. If these did not stop out of curiosity, as most of them did, they could be cornered in any one of a fan of narrow channels and small islands and shoal-water spots a few miles downstream. Cave in Rock was occupied at various times by various bands of outlaws, and of course there were all sorts of stories about hidden treasure there. It is now an Illinois state park.[40]

Aaron Burr and Peter sailed past this place without incident, and soon they were calling again upon Major General James Wilkinson, at St. Louis now.

The United States at the time was paying its army privates $3 a month, out of which 90¢ was deducted for sundry funds. It paid sergeants $3.60, lieutenants $22, captains $30. Whatever it allowed its major generals for expenses, for entertainment, Wilkinson exceeded this. Wilkinson presently was not only commander-in-chief of the United States Army, he was also governor of the vast, almost uninhabited territory of Louisiana, all the original Purchase north of the thirty-third parallel of latitude,[41] south of which was the Territory of Orleans. A big spender, he now had *two* expense accounts, and he was always in trouble with the government about them. At St. Louis, where they were to confer quietly for several more weeks, Aaron Burr was treated well by his host—the best food, the finest wines, music with every meal.

When he sailed away, to go back up the Ohio to Pittsburgh, and thence by land to Washington again, everything was all settled—everything, that is, except how to get the money.

18

"I gasconade not"

WHEN HE WENT WEST the next time—"never to return," in his own words—he took with him his beloved daughter, Theodosia. This could have been considered a good sign, for it is unlikely that he would ever expose her to any manner of frontier fracas—he loved her too much.

He was all bubble and bounce; he was effervescent. To those who had watched him in recent months as he went about Washington and Philadelphia trying to raise funds— it was from Philadelphia that they left, early in August—there seemed little enough reason for optimism. The British ambassador, Anthony Merry, a strong pro-Burr man, and other friends who had agreed to try to raise $110,000 from England plus the use of two or three warships off the mouth of the Mississippi, had been obliged to report a failure. The younger Pitt had died, and Charles James Fox, who succeeded him at the head of "the cabinet of all the talents," would have nothing to do with the Burr project, whatever it was. Burr in Washington had tried in vain to interest, for prestige purposes, certain public heroes—Truxtun, Decatur, Eaton of Derna. He had even approached the Spanish ambassador, Caso Yrujo, which was surely as far as effrontery could go. Yrujo, a jumping jack of a man, turned him down with exquisite politeness. Secretly, Yrujo told his government that he believed Aaron Burr to be an agent of the English, little knowing how much Burr wished that he *was*.

It was a bad time for filibusters. Francisco Miranda, up from Venezuela, had been back and forth in England and the United States raising money for a descent upon the South American coast, and the men who ordinarily would have had money to invest in such matters were found to be short when Aaron Burr came along, hat in hand.

The orotund warrior Wilkinson had written from St. Louis, using the cipher the two of them had devised. (They called it a cipher; but in fact it was, properly, neither a cipher nor a code, only a jumble of silly signs—a circle meant the President, a dash with two dots over it meant the secretary of state, and so forth—that any ten-year-old could have cracked in as many minutes.) He had, however, finished his letter with an unexpected burst of clarity. "I am ready," he had written.

Burr was a man of many attainments, but his greatest asset was his affability. He could charm the birds down out of the trees; but he had to be *there* to do it; he could not operate effectively at long-distance. His letters to Theodosia are classics, but as a letter writer usually he was more polished than persuasive. When he had come back up the Ohio from the lower Mississippi the previous fall it was New York financiers, friends of his, that he most wished to see; for here, after all, was his home town; but that murder warrant having to do with Hamilton's death still stood, and New York was closed to him. In a room with those men he would have been irresistible. From afar he could be refused, and he was.

He had perhaps $50,000 in his war chest when he set forth from Philadelphia, not much for a man who hoped to conquer an empire; but he had hope in his heart.

It is true that his son-in-law, John Alston, also was a member of the party, and Alston, a South Carolina planter, was one of the richest men in America. But Alston's wealth was all in land, and he'd just had two seasons of drought, so that, though rich, he was cashless.

Yet Aaron Burr did not worry. Already a westerner in spirit, he obeyed the old western admonition: when in doubt promote another land deal. He had, up his sleeve, so to speak, the Bastrop Grant.

Carondelet, the last Spanish governor of Louisiana, had, just before the French took over, ceded to Filipe Neri, Baron de Bastrop, a little matter of 1,200,000 acres in northern Orleans Territory, as it was now, along the Washita River. Though nobody in any way connected with this mighty deal ever had been there, it was generally understood that here was good land, rich land. The Spanish authorities never had endorsed the grant, never having been given time to; nor had the French, in the course of their twenty days of sovereignty, the second time 'round; nor had the United States since the American take-over. So the title was a shaky one at best. Yet it *was* good land—everybody said so. A Shelby County, Kentucky, lawyer, Charles Lynch, had somehow got control of three-fifths of the Bastrop Grant, and Aaron Burr, borrowing the money, of course, had purchased half of Lynch's claim. Burr, therefore, believed that in effect he owned 400,000 acres. He was already apportioning these when he left Philadelphia. His agents, who were recruiting men and building boats and gathering supplies in the upper Ohio valley, had been authorized to offer the proper volunteers twelve dollars a month apiece, and their clothes and keep for six months, *and* 150 acres of Louisiana. The agents were busy at this.

The recruits, so far, were largely young and husky easterners, lads from good families. Nothing was said about weapons, nothing about gunpowder; and this is remarkable. In all previous enlistment drives in the west the gun, usually a rifle though sometimes a musket, was taken for granted. The man was a gun, the gun the man. Customarily he was called upon to supply his own powder and ball as well, at least in the beginning. But nothing was said about this by

Aaron Burr's recruiters. Some of the men they signed up—a few, anyway—must have had weapons with them, but this was true of any group and certainly did not indicate a war-like intent. Most of them seemed to be going along just for the fun of it.

What *was* Burr up to? The whole country was asking this, and nobody seemed to know the answer. It is quite possible that he didn't know himself. He might have been playing the thing by ear, taking it as it came along, as it unfolded. There was nothing *blatantly* secretive about him. He *seemed* open and frank. He spoke on all sorts of public occasions, for he was given many a welcoming reception, many a banquet; but he really never said anything. Nor was this accountable merely by the politician in him. He had always been a reticent man.

Blennerhassett Island, located in the Ohio just below Marietta, was some three miles long, very narrow. Burr had visited the place twice the previous year, once on the way downstream, again on the way up, viewing the famous mansion, the celebrated gardens, but on neither occasion had he met the master, Harman Blennerhassett, a nearsighted little fellow who could play various musical instruments. Blennerhassett fell an instant victim to the Burr magic, flattening himself at the colonel's feet. An incorrigible dreamer, and anything but a businessman, he had been on Blennerhassett or at nearby Cincinnati for eight years, and there was very little left of the money he had first brought from Ireland. What there was, of course, was Burr's.

Blennerhassett, and his wife, and even more their servants, might indeed have injured the colonel's cause, whatever it was, by their carelessness of talk in company. They were hopeless romancers, all of them, and it was at about this time that vague, glittering rumors about plans for the crowning of Emperor Aaron I were first mentioned, as well as references to Princess Theodosia and the heir apparent, little Prince Aaron Burr Alston.

Burr himself was a careful drinker, a social drinker, and

not easily trapped into telling anything he shouldn't tell; but some of his followers were otherwise.

There was in the Lexington, Kentucky, district a federal attorney by the name of Joseph Hamilton Daveiss, who was young, handsome, and hotheaded. He was also a Federalist, one of the few still to be found in that part of the country, and perhaps for this reason the alarming reports of an uprising that he forwarded to the President did not deeply impress that personage. Daveiss went ahead on his own. He applied to federal Judge Harry Innes, of Frankfort, for a warrant to arrest Colonel Burr on charges of planning to invade Mexico and to separate the eastern from the western states. Innes, who happened to be entertaining his old friend Aaron Burr at that time—the judge was a member of the so-called Kentucky Committee of Correspondence, and deeply involved in the Spanish Conspiracy—likewise was not impressed. He said that it was a grand-jury matter. So Daveiss went to the grand jury.

Burr hired Henry Clay, who was twenty-nine and had just been appointed to the United States Senate (he would be thirty, as the Constitution requires, by the time he got to Washington and was inducted). Clay made Burr swear, first, that he was not planning anything detrimental to the United States. Then Clay went before the grand jury.

The hearing, which was public, was a delight to all Kentuckians, for Clay and Daveiss were bitter enemies. Once they had actually faced each other on the field of honor, and bloodshed had been prevented only because of the physical intervention of friends of both men. Daveiss and Clay, however, refused to shake hands afterward, and they were still not talking when the Burr affair came up. Frontiersmen reveled in such encounters.

There was a great deal of name-calling, but the grand jury elected to believe Henry Clay, and it not only exonerated Burr of all the charges against him but issued a statement

praising him for his patriotism. Burr's followers had this statement published as a handbill, which they distributed.

Jefferson, in the White House, was more concerned than
he appeared to be. After all, if New Orleans was in unfriendly
hands a breakaway of the Ohio Valley states could be expected, and then what would happen to that beautiful new
Louisiana Purchase? Jefferson watched Burr's progress with
a wary eye. He even sent a spy after the colonel, a quiet man
named Graham, a civilian, who as he dropped down the Ohio
quietly approached the small groups of young men who were
coming over the mountains for the purpose of joining Burr,
and talked them into returning to their homes.

Burr must have wondered what had happened to those
men. He was not to learn until much later.

He was careful, with what he had, to abstain from any
show of military might. Where he camped there were no
sentries posted, no drills, no bugle calls. The few guns seen
were being used only in shooting for the pot, a common
practice.

Later in December, when at last he pulled away from
Cumberland Island, where the Cumberland River empties
into the Ohio, he was clearly behind whatever schedule he
might have had. He had only eleven boats, one of them used
for supplies. Others were being built nearby, but he decided
to go without them. Judging from the boat-building orders
his agents had given he had expected to have a force of
about fifteen hundred men. Actually he had only about sixty
to seventy men when he left Cumberland Island; but he was
all smiles.

Had he counted on being joined by the United States
Army at about this time? It is not unlikely. If so, he was to
be disappointed.

Wilkinson had decided to get out. He did not like the
way the thing was going—or not going. Besides, it looked as
if he might soon have a real war on his hands, for the United

States and Spain were snarling at each other with more than their accustomed asperity. Spaniards—Spanish officers driving Mexican men—had crossed the Sabine River. Wilkinson, as commander-in-chief, hurried to the spot. At least he *said*, in his report, that he had hurried; though there were those who pointed out that three months was a mighty long time to take getting from St. Louis to Natchitoches. Probably he had not yet made up his mind about his erstwhile partner, Aaron Burr, whether to sell him out completely or to play innocent of the whole affair. He decided to sell him out.

It was at Natchitoches that he negotiated with the colonel in charge of the Mexican troops a treaty known as the Neutral Ground Treaty, by which each side promised not to go to the very banks of the Sabine until the matter should be clarified by higher authorities. This treaty was admittedly a stopgap. It was to cause complications later,[42] but for the present at least it averted hostilities.

It was at Natchitoches, too, that General Wilkinson, October 21, stabbed his friend Burr in the back. He did this in the form of a blistering letter addressed to the President and warning him and everybody else that a vast army of rogues and renegades was coming down the Mississippi and was about to engulf New Orleans.

"This," the general told the President, "is indeed a deep, dark, and widespread conspiracy, embracing the young and the old, the Democrat and the Federalist, the native and the foreigners, the patriot of '76 and the exotic of yesterday, the opulent and the needy, the 'ins' and the 'outs'; and I fear it will receive strong support in New Orleans from a quarter little suspected . . ."

He never mentioned Aaron Burr. He didn't have to.

"I gasconade not when I tell you that in such a cause I shall glory to give my life in the service of my country; for I verily believe such an event to be probable, because, should seven thousand men descend from the Ohio—and this is the calculation—they will bring with them the sympathies and good wishes of that country, and none but friends can be afterward prevailed on to follow them. With my handful of veterans, however gallant, it is improbable I shall be able to withstand such a disparity of numbers."

Jefferson called a special meeting of the cabinet, and they considered this message. They all knew that General Wilkinson had a tendency to exaggerate. But—he was *there*. He was on the spot, some thousand miles away, and there might be no time to study his report in detail and check its various points. Mr. Jefferson, to be sure, once had advocated the right of states to drop out of the Union any time they thought themselves wronged; but that had been before he was President, and before he had bought Louisiana. Such behavior now must not be permitted. He issued a proclamation calling upon all and sundry to arrest any who participated in any manner of uprising against the Union or against Mexico. Once again Burr was not mentioned by name, though nobody doubted that it was he who was meant.

The very day that President Jefferson staged his special cabinet meeting and issued this proclamation Wilkinson was riding into New Orleans. With his "handful of veterans" he might easily have routed the skimpy Spanish army on the Sabine, which was perilously far from its base, but he had other things to think of. There was his Spanish pension, for instance. Perhaps more important, certainly more immediate, was the need for magnifying the Burr menace. Wilkinson breathed fire, he snorted smoke. He shouted that there might be an inner-city revolt at any hour, perhaps even a servile revolt. He tried to get Governor Claiborne to declare martial law and to suspend the habeas corpus. Claiborne refused; whereupon General Wilkinson did these things himself, though he had no authority to. He pleaded the emergency.

In the Crescent City, afterward, they were to refer to it as a Reign of Terror. Sentries were everywhere, each sentry a spy. A curfew was imposed. Men who were believed to have even the remotest connection with Colonel Burr were unceremoniously seized, clapped into irons, and shipped out of town without any sort of hearing. Polysyllabic proclamations were posted everywhere; and if, in the light of later events, the Orléanais were able, some of them, to laugh a little at the noisy goings-on of those enfevered weeks while Wilkinson ruled, at the time assuredly they found it no laughing matter.

At Fort Massac, built in 1794 on the north bank of the Ohio about thirty-seven or thirty-eight miles from the Mississippi, Burr and his brave young desperadoes paused to pass the time of day—the last day, incidentally, of 1806—with the commanding officer, a Captain Bissell, who very kindly lent them the services of a sergeant, to whom he issued a twenty-day furlough, as guide. Two days later, when news of the President's proclamation reached Fort Massac, Bissell was to wish that he had not been so helpful; but that was two days later.

On New Year's Day of 1807 the small flotilla emerged into the Father of Waters. It paused at New Madrid, another United States Army post, only to be waved smilingly on. A few days later, January 4, it tied up at Chickasaw Bluffs, Tennessee. The commanding officer there, Lieutenant Jacob Jackson, was a son of one of Burr's best friends, and they had a long and friendly talk. So enthusiastic about an attack upon Mexico did young Jackson become that he wrote the war department resigning his commission and accepted $150 from Colonel Burr for use in raising a company of volunteers. Once again, as at Massac, as at New Madrid, the President's proclamation had not yet arrived.

January 10 the "brigands"—as Wilkinson called them in his reports—tied up at Bayou Pierre, some 30 miles above Natchez, and here for the first time Burr heard about the President's proclamation: he read it in the *Mississippi Gazette.*

Here too he learned what no doubt he already suspected —that Wilkinson had turned against him. He heard about the

Reign of Terror in New Orleans and he could guess its purpose.

The Mississippi militia had been called out. Burr had picked up a few more young men since leaving Cumberland Island; he might have had almost a hundred now; but even if all his boys had been armed, and even if he were willing to give battle to fellow Americans, he would not have had a chance. He was outnumbered, with more militiamen coming in all the time.

He knew that if Wilkinson ever got his hands on him he would have him sent to New Orleans, there to face a drumhead court-martial and immediately afterward a firing squad. Wilkinson would thus obliterate all evidence of his own complicity in the expedition, all the while pleading that emergency.

(The General indeed already had ordered a party of soldiers in civilian clothes to kidnap Burr, and they had started for Washington, then the capital of Mississippi. They had no warrant, but they were all armed. They had been promised their expenses in any case and $5,000 if they brought in their man. Burr himself probably never heard of this party.)[43]

Burr was no fool. He knew when he was beaten. He gathered his boys together and addressed them. They were welcome to settle upon any part of the Bastrop Grant they could reach, he told them, though Wilkinson's men already were blocking this off. He apologized for not being able to pay them. Any clothes or gear they had drawn they could keep. They could sell the boats and divide the proceeds as they pleased. (In fact, they were to get very good prices for the eleven boats, which were well made, much better craft than any ever seen in those parts before.) Again, he was sorry. Good-bye.

He borrowed a horse and some old clothes and disappeared into the wilderness.

A reward of $2,000 was offered for his capture.

A few of his closest followers—Comfort Tyler, Davis Floyd, Harman Blennerhassett—were arrested and held for a little while; but nobody could think of an appropriate charge to bring against them, and they were soon released. The "privates," the boys, broke up. A few worked their way back up the river, but most of them settled down there in the Natchez-Baton Rouge country. They were not common Kaintucks. They were hard-working, courteous young men, and well liked by their neighbors.

An alert registrar of lands far down on the road to Pensacola a week later recognized a passerby because of his shortness and slight build, and also because of the beautifully polished boot that showed beneath ragged pantaloons, and he had him arrested. The arresting agent was a promising young Army officer, Lieutenant Edmund Pendleton Gaines,[44] who arranged to have the prisoner taken to Richmond, Virginia, where he arrived March 26, and where he was to be tried.

That trial, presided over by Chief Justice John Marshall, was a classic. The government brought Wilkinson east to testify against the defendant, and he made a clown of himself with his stentorian snortings and his pyrotechnical if not always grammatical tirades. Aaron Burr had hired some brilliant attorneys himself, but he didn't really need them, for he was quite capable of taking care of himself in any courtroom, and he made fools of the prosecution. In a blaze of publicity such as the nation never had known before, he was acquitted; yet everybody really believed that he was guilty, and his career, at least in America, was at an end. He sneaked away to Europe.

The dust settled. The last tiny echoes melted into silence in faraway corners. But the mouth of the Mississippi remained free. The back door of America remained open.

19

He Did Everything Wrong

IMPERIALISM HAS a toxic action. It gets speedily into the bloodstream, spreading. No sooner had the Americans so unexpectedly annexed those millions of acres west of the Mississippi than they started to clamor for more—specifically, the Floridas. To have Louisiana was heady; but to have Louisiana without East and West Florida seemed, somehow, unfair.

To ask for more than you can expect to get, and to keep asking for it, in a hurt voice, is one of the primary rules of treaty-making. Throughout the long negotiations in Paris between the Americans and French on one side and the British on the other, in preparation for bringing to an end the American Revolutionary War, for instance, Benjamin Franklin, ordinarily the most benign and undemanding of men, had determinedly insisted that not only Nova Scotia but also all of Canada be made over to the new republic, which had not a smidgen of title to either. He did this with a straight face. The claim, itself impertinent, was a diplomatic weapon in his hand, and though he did not swing it in a menacing manner he made sure that the British never lost track of the fact that it was *there*.

Such devices were common in diplomacy; but ordinarily they were dropped when the sought end had been obtained, as Dr. Franklin dropped his claim to Canada once the British had granted American independence and full American control of the Northwest Territory.

In the case of the Louisiana Purchase an opposite result was to be noted. Not only did the United States fail to drop its clamor for the Floridas once the vastly greater territory of Louisiana had been attached, but it increased that demand. The nation seemed to have gone land-mad. Before it had even begun to devise a plan for governing all it possessed, it was crying for more.

It seemed *unnatural* that the Floridas, hemmed in on the north and west by the United States, and held only by palsied, tottering Spain, should not become part of the new republic. This was particularly true because so many Americans were drifting into those territories, and especially into West Florida, which already seemed more American than Spanish. The United States indeed had enough claims on the Floridas to seize them, if only she had also fifty thousand bayonets. Napoleon Bonaparte had taken over whole nations in Europe with slighter excuses.

President Jefferson, once he had been able to quell his own trepidation about the legality of annexing Louisiana, looked swiftly in all directions for further land to appropriate, and he was in love with the Floridas.

All residents of the southern states felt the same way, for the Floridas were virtually within their arms already. New York and the New England states were not so enthusiastic, fearing as they did that the southern states were waxing too strong in Congress.

Jefferson always hated the thought of war, and he planned to get these provinces without recourse to it. Godoy, the Prince of Peace, was back in power in Madrid, after a short spell of private life, and Godoy always had been a good friend of the United States, a man who actually seemed to *enjoy* standing up to Bonaparte; so Jefferson was hopeful.

It was a Federalist, Ambassador Livingston, who came up with the most dazzling excuse for the annexation of Florida. It was an excuse that had all the intricate, involuted fascination of a spider web, and just about that much strength.

Livingston pointed out that France once had owned all of Louisiana, which was then taken to mean the entire stretch of territory between the Alleghenies and the Rockies, on both sides of the Mississippi. When, at the end of the Seven Years' War, Great Britain was offered by France, the loser, her choice between the vast land of Louisiana and the two Floridas, she unhesitatingly took the Floridas. *But*—and here was where Mr. Livingston made his clever point—East and West Florida, certainly West Florida anyway, remained indisputably a part of Louisiana. At the end of the American Revolution, thanks to Gálvez's conquests, Great Britain had been obliged to cede the Floridas to Spain, though in fact they remained, unknown to the rest of the world, an integral part of Louisiana. Spain, then, when it retroceded Louisiana to France had retroceded the Floridas as well, and France when she sold Louisiana to the United States had also sold the Floridas. All this had been done unwittingly, according to Mr. Livingston. As Henry Adams was to put it,[45] Livingston "was forced at last to maintain that Spain had retroceded West Florida to France without knowing it, that France had sold it to the United States without suspecting it, that the United States had bought it without paying for it, and that neither France nor Spain, although the original contracting parties, were competent to decide the meaning of their own contract."

This inspired bit of legal fluff, coming as it did from a Federalist, would have passed unnoticed had not the republican James Monroe adopted it, urging it upon the secretary of state, James Madison, and the President, Thomas Jefferson, who succumbed to its charms, cheering it as the answer to America's territorial problems.

All four of these men—Jefferson, Madison, Livingston, Monroe—were members of the bar. To them had been divulged the secret of the arcane rites that were the law, and they, the anointed ones, the high priests, had brought down from their own private Sinai their own stone tablets engraved with whatever they wished.

There were still a few laymen left in the halls of Congress, not to mention New England, and the Livingston thesis, too precious for the likes of them, did not gain much ground. Jefferson had to look elsewhere for a justification for grabbing these southern climes when the right time came.

Livingston's preposterous claim extended east to the Perdido, the "Lost River" of the Spaniards,[46] which unassuming stream runs into the Gulf about halfway between Mobile and Pensacola. The rest of Florida, including the whole peninsula, East Florida, an arid wasteland where few men lived, did not vitally concern those in Washington. It did, however, greatly concern the planters of Georgia, who kept crying for its takeover. Georgians did not crave the land itself—who would want that flat dreary place?—but they feared to see it in foreign hands because it made a sanctuary for runaway slaves. Of all the large slave-owning nations Spain was the most liberal (as the United States was the *least* liberal) in her laws regarding the Peculiar Institution, the least harsh in her treatment of Negroes. When slaves escaped from the plantations of Georgia and South Carolina, if they were well directed they made their way to the Florida frontier. Once in St. Augustine they were safe. Spain would not return them. Georgia spluttered and swore, but she was not strong enough to go to war with Spain by herself, and the federal government still held off.

West Florida was a more immediate goal. It was filling with Americans, rough frontiersmen who had no fondness for the dons, and who were forever kicking up dust storms. At last, September 26, 1810, a group of them, in convention assembled, issued their own declaration of independence, probably the briefest on record. The land they laid claim to was between the Mississippi and the Pearl rivers, and it was largely American already, though stubborn Spain still considered it hers. The United States recognized the new patch of sovereignty, which it decreed should become a part of the territory of Orleans, soon to become the state of Louisiana. December 7 of that same year Governor Claiborne at St. Francisville, the capital of this small place, raised the Stars and Stripes. No war resulted.[47]

Congress could take incidents like this in its stride. However, when it came time to admit Louisiana—once the province of Orleans—there was a very great hubbub indeed. The remaining Federalists fairly howled, and one of them, Josiah Quincy of Massachusetts, hurled at the House some of its most memorable lines:

"I am compelled to declare it as my deliberate opinion, that, if this bill passes, the bonds of this Union are virtually dissolved; that the States which compose it are free from their moral obligations, and that, as it will be the right of all, so it will be the duty of some, to prepare definitely for a separation—amicably if they can, violently if they must."

Just as Patrick Henry in his celebrated speech before the Virginia House of Burgesses was interrupted when he reached what seemed a perilous edge, "Caesar had his Brutus, Charles the First his Cromwell, and King George—" by shouts of "Treason! Treason!" so on this occasion, and at this point, was Josiah Quincy halted. The Speaker of the House, a Jeffersonian, called him to order. There was an immediate appeal from the floor, and a vote was taken, and the Speaker's decision was reversed. Josiah Quincy went on with his speech.

Yet the motion was passed by a firm majority, and Louisiana, April 30, 1812, became the eighteenth state of the Union.

This helped; but there were many other bits of unfinished business on the government's desk, and one of them was the awkward question of what to do with James Wilkinson.

He had made a monumental fool of himself at the Burr trial. The government probably couldn't have convicted Burr anyway, but Wilkinson with his struttings and his splutterings and the querulous clacking of his sword made the outcome certain. Easterners never really had seen the man before, and they stood appalled. Was *this* the commander-in-chief of our army? It was hard to believe. Laughing at generals in general was not a common practice at the time, and indeed Wilkinson can be said to have started it. Until his absurd appearance in Richmond generals usually had been thought of somewhat fearfully, at least with respect. But Wilkinson, a ripsnorting liar, burlesqued his own profession. "Bombastes Furioso," the literati called him. The populace took a hint from Washington Irving, a bright young man who had covered the Burr trial for one of the New York papers, and who was to put James Wilkinson into his *Diedrich Knickerbocker's History of New York*—which book, incidentally, gave that city the name of Father Knickerbocker—unmistakably as General Jacobus von Poffenberg: "booted to the middle, sashed to the chin, collared to the ears, whiskered to the teeth." This picture, this comic figure, was accepted by the public, which was unfortunate, for, though the man undeniably was funny, he was dangerous as well; there was poison in him.

Aaron Burr had become a blur of rumors wafted back from abroad, tales of affairs with incandescent duchesses, of discussions with philosophers, of pitiful attempts to raise money for impossibly grand projects; [48] but James Wilkinson had to be taken care of. The United States Army always had been chary of high titles; it was determined not to be one of those small-republic defense bodies in which the colonels outnumbered the sergeants, the generals the captains, and it was hard even to find a private. George Washington himself had held only the rank of major general throughout the Revolution and also throughout his two terms of office as President. It was not until 1798 that he was made a lieutenant general, and he never actually served in this capacity. When the War of 1812 broke out the army was faced with the embarrassing fact that the soiled eagle James Wilkinson not only was a major general but the *only* major general on active duty. Since he wouldn't resign and refused to die, he had to be used in some conspicuous command.

"Free trade and sailors' rights" was the reason given for the war, though it is worthy of remark that the New England states, home of most of the sailors and the headquarters for by far the largest portion of American trade, were bitterly opposed. As far as residents of the Ohio Valley were concerned—and they were known as Hawks or War Hawks, though there was no group designated as Doves—the chief reason for the war was a chance to snatch a huge chunk of, or perhaps all of, Canada. Millions of acres—think of the land deals these could represent! An invasion of Canada therefore was the first thing on the military's agenda, and James Wilkinson was perforce appointed to lead it.

He did everything wrong. The very first invasion—there were to be others—was an unmitigated failure. Major General Wilkinson, though nobody ever accused him of *stealing* anything, was brought up on charges, all sorts of charges, and it took the army years to decide what to do with him. He was at last permitted to resign with the rank of lieutenant colonel at full pay for life—$3,500 a year. He went to Mexico. His Spanish pension had long since ceased, but now, in his sixties, he began to learn Spanish. He was at last what he had always wanted to be—a buyer and seller of land. He dealt indefatigably in real estate, specializing in sections of the Mexican state of Texas. At one time he owned all the land that the present city of Galveston rests on; yet when he died, December 28, 1825, a victim of the climate and of opium, he was a comparatively poor man, and long since forgotten. He is buried in Mexico City.

CHAPTER

20

Death at the Edge of the Swamp

GREAT BRITAIN, AS THE British saw it, for some time had been single-handedly fighting the foes of liberty in the form of Napoleon Bonaparte and his minions. The United States, in view of its resounding professions, should have been fighting at her side, instead of sneakily declaring war on her. The United States, in the British belief, had taken advantage of the valiant all-out stand against tyranny to try to rip off a piece of Canada, something it would never have dared if England had not been so bitterly preoccupied elsewhere. This was a dirty trick; and when Boney had been taken care of, it was vowed at Whitehall, the United States would be punished for it.

The echoes of the cannonading at Waterloo had scarcely whimpered away, the dust had scarcely settled and the last limp soldier been buried, when Great Britain, in July of that year 1814, started to prepare for this punishment, this knock-out blow.

Until now Britain had done little about the war across the sea, a side issue. Small detachments of third- and fourth-rate war vessels had ranged the American coast, the 2,805 exposed miles that stretched between Passamaquoddy Bay and the mouths of the Mississippi, easily chasing the ships of the little United States Navy up various rivers, where they were to remain for the rest of the war. The several invasions of Canada had been bloodily thrown back. Amphibious forces had harassed eastern ports and the capital city of Washington, which had been burned. Now the serious work would be started.

A fleet was to be assembled in Negril Bay at the western tip of Jamaica and, together with transports packed with the veterans of Salamanca, Badajoz, Vitoria, and of Waterloo itself, was to descend crushingly upon the Crescent City.

The commanding officer of this mighty force already had been selected: he was Major General Robert Ross, the same who had led the smashing attack upon Washington, who had burned the White House, causing President Madison to scurry away into the hinterland. Ross, however, forestalled this appointment by getting himself killed in the course of an unsuccessful attack upon Baltimore. Lieutenant General Lord Hill then was considered, as was Vice Admiral Sir Alexander Cochrane, who indeed was appointed commander of the naval arm of the expedition, but at last there was picked the impressive figure of Major General Sir Edward Pakenham.

Pakenham (pronounced PAY-ken-em) was only thirty-eight years old. He was in superb health and had been in the army all his life. More important, he was a brother-in-law of the Duke of Wellington.

On November 26, after a long, slow, but determined buildup, the fleet at Negril Bay sailed, more than fifty vessels strong, flags flying, bands playing.

Four days before that, the commanding officer of United States Military District No. 7—Louisiana, Alabama, Mississippi, Tennessee, Kentucky—had mounted his horse at Mobile and started for New Orleans. He took his time. Had he been in a hurry he would have gone by boat, the inland waterway. The middle of the previous month he had been waited upon by a delegation of prominent New Orleans citizens who begged him to make a visit to the Crescent City and look after its defenses. These men had heard—everybody had heard by this time—of the fleet that was assembling off Jamaica. They believed that it was destined for New Orleans. The commanding officer of Military District No. 7 did not agree. He believed that Mobile would be the point of attack. Mobile was now in territory claimed by the United States under its own curious interpretation of the Louisiana Purchase treaty, though Spain did not acknowledge this.

The commanding officer was a pale, lank, skinny, sick man with a lantern jaw and an inflexible will, named Andrew Jackson. Not only was he the head of the Tennessee militia but, as a wartime measure, he had been made a major general of the regular United States Army, and his word in that part of the land was law. He was, essentially, a backwoodsman. Fearless, tough, nevertheless he knew nothing about conventional warfare. He was conscious of this ignorance, and of course he sought to conceal it.

The Seventh Military District had not been slighted. When the war department spread the United States Army thin across the country it skimped New England, for the British, who hoped that the New England states would secede from the Union, as they were threatening to do, were not enforcing their blockade there, and certainly would not invade any part of the place. But the Seventh District got more manpower than any other: five regular infantry regiments—the 2nd, 3rd, 7th, 39th, and 44th—besides 350 artillerists. Jackson should not have complained on that score, though undoubtedly he did, for no general ever thinks that he has enough men.

New Orleans would be a splendid prize. Besides its strategic position in control of the mouth of the Mississippi, it was crowded with supplies the British blockade had not permitted to get out of the country. Its warehouses contained cotton and sugar to the estimated value of $17,500,000, be-

ANDREW JACKSON—SKINNY, SICK, INFLEXIBLE

sides tobacco, hemp, and lead which, together with the shipping tied up there, might have been worth $2,500,000 more.
Even so, General Jackson did not believe that New Orleans
would be hit. Mobile was his choice.

Because he thought it to be a part of his duty, he did
examine the downriver defenses.

Balize, the old French fort at the very mouth of the
river, the principal mouth, was in ruins. Two other French
strongholds, not in very good shape but mounting a few
workable cannons, St. Philip and Bourbon, were to be found
opposite each other about fifty miles up from the Gulf. Assuming that an invading fleet got past these it would surely
be stopped at English Turn, a wicked bend in the river only
sixteen miles below New Orleans. Besides the guns mounted
there the place could readily be defended by the sloop-of-war
Louisiana, which mounted sixteen long 24-pounders, and the
schooner-of-war *Carolina,* fourteen guns. The very year that
the war had started, the year after which it was named, 1812,
the first steamboat had reached New Orleans from Pittsburgh; and now that same vessel was making the run two or
even three times a year; but there were no steamboats on
the lower river, and certainly the British had none. To *sail*
around English Turn was an elaborate and tricky maneuver,
and it took time, and no matter how fast the craft might be,
and no matter how well handled, it could be pounded to
pieces before it got halfway.

New Orleans, then, seemed safe enough from the south.

The south*west* approach was smugglers' territory, an
aquatic maze of bayous, rivers, and cypress swamps by
means of which a fair-sized boat could make its way from the
Gulf to a point right across the river from the Crescent City—
if it had engaged the right guide. The British already had in-
vestigated the southwestern possibility, offering money and
a navy commission to Jean Lafitte, who, with his brother
Pierre, in jail just then, controlled the racket. Jean Lafitte
stalled them, and went to Andrew Jackson, offering his

services if his brother was freed and both men were promised a federal pardon for past sins. Jackson agreed. Jackson was taking anybody he could get.

The south*eastern* approach, another all-water one, would be by Lake Borgne—not really a lake at all but a lagoon—and after that a series of snaky bayous that extended (if you knew the way) almost to the Mississippi at a point *above* English Turn, a point about halfway between the Turn and the city of New Orleans. This would call for expert local pilots, such as the British navy could hardly be expected to provide, and a large fleet of shallow-draft boats. General Jackson did not seriously consider it.

He favored the northern approach, by way of the Chef Menteur road and the plains of Gentilly. It would have been much longer, though certainly not as wet. It would have taken the British invaders more than fifty miles inland, away from their base, the fleet, and through swamp-treacherous country over which it would not be possible to drag field pieces or any appreciable amount of supplies. Nevertheless General Jackson, who was no expert in supply matters, believed that the British, if they came at all, would come by this route; and he posted a large portion of his command across the Chef Menteur road.

The British did in fact enter Lake Borgne, at the far end of which, blocking the entrance to the New Orleans-leading bayous, was a cluster of United States Navy gunboats. There were five of these, low, rickety things, under the command of Lieutenant Thomas Ap Catesby Jones. They couldn't have kept out a catfish.

"The Gun Boats on the Lakes will prevent the British from approaching in that quarter," General Jackson wrote to James Monroe, who, besides being secretary of state, was now acting as secretary of war. General Jackson did not know much about naval matters.

The British fleet, anchored off Cat Island and Ship Island at the entrance of Lake Borgne, could not reach these gunboats, which were in shallow water; so heavily manned barges were sent out.

The result came as no surprise. The Americans fought gallantly and well, but in a very short time they were all dead or prisoners.

Even when he heard that the British were off the entrance to Lake Borgne General Jackson did not worry. He wrote to Secretary Monroe that he was sure that this was only a "a Faint." He did, however, send a corporal's guard out to a tiny fishing village located on Bienvenu Bayou near where it emptied into Lake Borgne, from where a man could watch the fleet, reporting any suspicious movement. The squad arrived there—the village was so small that it had no name, being only a huddle of huts—late the following afternoon, to find the place deserted. There was nothing startling about this. The men might often stay out fishing all night. The American soldiers made themselves comfortable, and went to sleep. When they awoke they found that they were completely surrounded by British soldiers.

The British, as soon as the gunboats had been brushed aside, penetrated Bienvenu Bayou as far as the village. The fishermen were all Spanish, and had no love for the newcomers to that section of their watery world—the Yankees. The British were prepared for this, and had Spanish speakers in their midst. They could offer real money, gold, not just promises; and the fishermen all signed on as pilots and guides.

The level of the water, from the Mississippi itself to the tiniest bayou, was exceptionally low, lower than anybody could remember its having been before; and this was a condition that would work against the British, making it hard for them to float their boats. Some of the irrigation ditches and even some of the bayous indeed were dry: they had muddy bottoms but no water.

To hamper further any British approach, General Jackson had ordered that trees be felled across all the principal waterways of the district, especially those that led north to the Chef Menteur road. Why this was not done in the case of Bayou Bienvenu, and why the corporal's squad had taken so long to get there, will never be known.

The American prisoners did the best they could to modify their failure. Questioned separately, they were as one in testifying that General Jackson had about twenty thousand men waiting just outside New Orleans. In fact Jackson had only about one-tenth that number, and those badly scattered.

Boats provided by the British navy were everywhere. Redcoats were everywhere too, as were sailors, and marines, virtually all of them veterans. They numbered 1,688 rank-and-file, besides the officers, besides the fishermen-guides, and they had been designated for this occasion as the 22nd Light Brigade.

They made no attempt at secrecy. They pushed through that misty wilderness for a few miles, and abruptly, a little before noon on the 23rd of December, a hot muggy day, they came upon an open space backed by cane fields and the river, the Mississippi itself. There stood a rambling white plantation house, and slaves moved through and about it. A young man was seated on the veranda of that house, his feet on a rail, a straw hat tipped over his face, sound asleep. This was Gabriel Villeré, son of the plantation's owner, General de Villeré, commanding officer of the Louisiana militia, who was in the city on military business. Gabriel Villeré was himself a major in the militia, though not on duty at the moment. They had to shake him to wake him up and tell him that he was a prisoner.

Young Villeré, looking around to find his ancestral acres inundated with redcoats, and more appearing all the time, thought fast. They were only six miles from the center of New Orleans, and he knew that there wasn't a redoubt, a redan, a trench, a picket, in between.

He wrenched himself free, vaulted over the veranda rail, and ran like mad for the swamp.

They fired after him, but he made it.

They did not pursue him. He probably knew every inch of that swamp, which could engulf soldiers and sink them like dead leaves. Besides, what was the hurry? The city was theirs. It was only a stroll away.

Elsewhere in the world, at just this same time, in two other places, important meetings were being held.

In Ghent, Flanders, a diplomatic team of five Americans conferred with three Britishers, their purpose being peace. The Britishers were minor officials, the best men of the Foreign Office being engaged in the much more important treaty conference in Vienna, a conference that would redraw the whole map of Europe after the Napoleonic wars. The Americans were that country's best, a dedicated band. Knowing the impatience of their confreres, who mightily wished to be elsewhere, where the action was, the Americans delayed and delayed, until at last they persauded these lesser legates to agree to the principle of *uti possidetis*. In other words, everything would be as it had been before the war, a stunning victory for the Americans, who distinctly had "lost." Free trade and sailors' rights were not even mentioned at Ghent.

The other meeting was one of Federalists, and it was held in Hartford, Connecticut. There were only twenty-three delegates at first, though a few others drifted in, all of them New Englanders. The meeting elected as its president George Cabot of Massachusetts, a man who could be cautiously described as a mossback, who more than once had expressed abhorrence of democracy. The sessions of the Hartford Convention were secret, as had been the sessions of the Second Continental Congress that adopted the Declaration of Independence. Rumors about it swirled. The country, everybody agreed, teetered at the edge of chaos. It was virtually bankrupt. An enormous British army and naval force had been gathering for months just off Jamaica, and it was understood that it had sailed for New Orleans. If that city fell, so assuredly would the rest of the land. President Madison then would have no other choice but to resign, and it would be a case of what the French call *sauve qui peut,* every state for itself. The Hartford Convention delegates wished to be prepared for this.

At the Villeré plantation the ranking officer, Colonel Thornton, a salamander, was all for plunging ahead. The slaves, questioned, said as the soldier-prisoners had said, that there were twenty thousand armed men prepared to defend New Orleans. Thornton didn't believe them. But Thornton's superior, Major General John Keane, who now arrived at the plantation, did. The general pointed out that nobody, not even an idiot of a Yankee, would have left open a hole like this. It was an *invitation* to walk in. It was, Keane feared, a trap. The commander-in-chief, Major General Pakenham, the Iron Duke's brother-in-law, would be there any day now. They had been obliged to sail from Negril Bay without him, but they knew that he was close behind. Pakenham had been promised an earldom, and he carried in his wallet a commission appointing him Governor of Louisiana. All credit for the fall of the city would go to him, no matter what; but if there was a costly misstep in advance, the fault would be that of Major General Keane. Keane ordered a halt. The British pitched camp.

Gabriel Villeré, in the course of his run from the plantation to Jackson's headquarters at 106 Royal Street—and he *had* run, all the way—had picked up a friend, Dussau de la Croix, who could speak a little English, a language Major Villeré didn't know. This was a little after three o'clock in the afternoon.

Young De la Croix was so badly out of breath that he forgot much of his English, badly mispronouncing the rest, so that it was some time before he could make himself understood.

General Jackson rose, banging the table.

"By God, gentlemen, we'll fight them! Right now!'

He gathered every scrap of military force he could find, a heterogeneous bag, and with it went thundering down the road to the Villeré plantation. It was a foggy night.

What happened then could hardly be described as a battle. It was rather a brawl. Because of the fog many on both sides strayed from their units and became prisoners. Losses were about equal, and the British retained their camp. Nobody could be said to "have won" this tussle. The Americans, in fairly good order, fell back upriver a little to the Rodriguez Canal, a man-dug ditch ten feet wide and three-fourths of a mile long that stretched between swamp and river, where they established themselves. There was no water in the ditch, but the bottom was mud.

There were many things about the military art that Andrew Jackson did not know, but he *did* know how to fight. Faced with a foe, an enemy he could see, he had no doubts, no wavering. He was a happy man then.

The British took hogsheads of raw sugar from the Villeré and nearby Lacoste plantations, and they used these to protect not their infantry but their gunners. They were no good. Balls would smash them, scattering splinters. The men would try to eat the stinking raw stuff thus exposed, and it made them violently sick.

There were no rocks or stones in that low country, and no timber except the cypress fetched out of the swamp, a place the British avoided, for it was filled with shadowy Cherokees, Jackson's allies. The Americans had brought some boards from New Orleans, and also large numbers of cotton bales, for fortification. The cotton would stop a musket ball, but it all too rapidly caught fire from the Americans' guns. When this happened the men would tumble a burning bale down into the Rodriguez Canal, until the officers stopped this practice, because it would have made overleaping the canal that much easier for the British. Some of the bales then were torn to pieces, handfuls of the stuff being crammed under the soldiers' clothes against the cold of the nights. The remain-

THE BATTERIES OF COTTON BALES

ing bales were sent back to the reserves, who did the same thing with them.

Pakenham arrived, and he shook a grave head at what he saw. This was no place to stay, hemmed in by the swamp on one side, the levee and river on the other. Supplying it was a backbreaking job, for everything had to be hauled from the fleet. To go forward would mean a head-on attack against a strongly fortified position. To retreat was, of course, unthinkable.

Pakenham pointed out to his subordinates that this campaign was not being conducted properly. It was a rule of civilized warfare that each arm of the service should first eliminate its opposite number on the enemy's side—the cavalry should wipe out the cavalry, and so forth. There was no cavalry on either side on the plains below New Orleans, so Pakenham decreed that there should be an artillery duel. He brought up more guns and much more ammunition. December 28, all day, these spoke.

The Americans immediately answered them, and the Americans proved to be the better shots. The two war vessels in the river were helpful. A lucky British shot from behind the levee got the *Louisiana* right in the magazine, blowing her up, though all the men escaped by swimming; but the doughty little *Carolina* carried on.

The duel was emphatically an American success. The British artillery had been almost halved, while all American guns, except those aboard the *Louisiana*, were intact.

The line at the Rodriguez Canal had not been shaken.

There seemed to be nothing else for it but a frontal assault. Ever since Bunker Hill, forty years back, the best British military minds had devoted themselves to finding ways of avoiding a frontal assault. The thing was magnificent, but too expensive.

Admiral Cochrane came up with a daring plan to cut through the levee, flooding an irrigation ditch, the flood waters to be stopped by a previously built dam near the swamp. By this means—and it would have to be done at night, lest it draw American artillery fire—boats could be put into the Mississippi itself, which was about a mile wide at this point. Men under Colonel Thornton could be sent against a troublesome battery on the other side, and those guns could be turned against the Americans themselves, while the British charged the Rodriguez line.

The Mississippi, always an unaccountable stream, suddenly rose, as though at a nod from God. There was no apparent reason for this, certainly no *local* reason. It just happened, and on the very night when the British were tearing a hole in the levee. It broke the dam they had built. It doubled the work of launching the boats. It put Colonel Thornton two hours behind his schedule, for it carried him to a point lower on the river than he had planned, and, though he did knock out the troublesome battery, he could not turn the guns against the defenders of New Orleans, for the Americans had been given time to spike them.

The British infantry went in just the same, on January 8. They had never been more admirable, or more vulnerable. Their training told them to step *around* fallen men, rather than *over* them, as they advanced under fire; but they had no chance to practice this tactic, for men were not falling here and there, now and then, but in whole rows, in great wide fan-shaped swatches, as though cut down by a scythe.

The Sutherlanders, for example. They were the only Highland regiment, and the largest outfit, in the army, nine hundred strong. Something went wrong with their orders, and they were left stranded in an oblique position right before the middle of the Rodriguez line, where the Tennesseeans were. The Tennesseeans had rifles, not just muskets. By the time the confusion in orders was straightened out there were only 160 Sutherlanders left standing.

A few Britishers did reach the Rodriguez line, and got into the ditch. None of them got out again.

General Pakenham was knocked off his horse with four

THE BATTLE OF NEW ORLEANS

THE DEATH OF THE BRITISH GENERAL, EDWARD PAKENHAM

grapeshot wounds, any one of which would have been enough to kill him. He would never be an earl.

General Keane went down, and General Gibbs, both dead.

It all happened in just a few minutes. The British losses were 2,036, the American 21—8 killed, 13 wounded.

The only general left, Lambert, looked around the field. You could hardly tell the color of the mud from the prone redcoats and the lovely, dark green Sutherland tartan on the kilts. It was raining now. Lambert ordered a retreat.

The Americans already were scuttling across the Rodriguez Canal. They had not organized a pursuit. They were looking for souvenirs.

The war was over. It had not been a war of which either side could be proud; but if it had proved anything it had proved that the mouth of the Mississippi was indubitably, undeniably, and forever American.

Notes

1. As is well known, the Mississippi River, without asking anyone's permission, often changes its course. Thus the town of Delta, Mississippi, at one time was located three miles below Vicksburg, but in the 1870s the river took a sudden cutoff, and Delta found itself two miles *above* Vicksburg, or—as it was called in the days of James Willing—Walnut Hills, and, by the Spaniards, Los Nogales. Zadok Cramer, the first geographer of the Ohio-Mississippi route, gives the distance from the mouth of the Ohio to the city of New Orleans as 1,009 miles. Today, thanks to the United States Army engineering corps, it is 973 miles.

2. His portrait hangs in the Cabildo in New Orleans today. With his ice-blue eyes he looks like a bad man to challenge. It was said, though, that he had beautiful manners.

3. Caughey, *Louisiana Historical Quarterly,* January 1932. This is one of the few reliable descriptions of what southern historians generally call Willing's Raid. These historians, with very little evidence to go on, paint Willing as a monster, a Moloch intent upon destroying everything in his path. Words fail them—though they keep trying—when they

come to tell of Willing's brutality. Yet the "raid" was a legitimate and duly commissioned martial enterprise, and the complaints of the ravaged ones, though shrill enough, centered largely upon the fact that Captain Willing was taking from men with whom, a little earlier, he had dined and supped. *That,* in their eyes, was unforgivable.

4. So they were customarily designated. In fact, at just this time the relationship was even closer. Carlos III of Spain was the uncle of young Louis XV of France.

5. There has been some dispute about his age when he became governor of Louisiana, the estimates ranging from twenty-one to thirty-one. He was probably in his upper twenties (Caughey, *Bernardo de Gálvez,* p. 68). He was not only young in years, he was young in spirit. He had exuberance and a quick charm. His youth—it could almost be called boyishness—showed up the brighter in contrast to the labored stodginess of the governor he had succeeded, old Luis de Unzaga y Amézaga.

6. "In its four hundred recorded years more men have died defending or conquering or exploiting this river than any other in North America." Carter, *Lower Mississippi,* p. 4.

7. Alden, *General Gage in America.*

8. "The Revolutionary War in the west might almost be called Clark's War . . . its boldest conceptions, its only great offensives, and its paramount achievement were distinctly his." Bodley, *George Rogers Clark,* p. 146.

9. Caughey, *Bernardo de Gálvez,* pp. 252–53. *See also* Caughey's articles in *Louisiana Historical Quarterly,* vol. 15 (1932), pp. 5–36, and vol. 16 (1933), pp. 57–83.

10. A five-hundred-foot notch in the mountains located about where the present states of Virginia, Tennessee, and Kentucky come together. The Chesapeake and Ohio Railroad was to utilize it.

11. Erie, Pennsylvania, today.

12. "When the pioneer set about his task of making the wilderness blossom like a rose, the instrument that he em-

ployed was an ax. He had nothing to offer in place of the beauty he destroyed . . . the frontier was 'a detestable place.' A clearing granulated with the stumps of trees, muddy crossroads (or dusty ones, according to the season), hogs rooting in the litter about the general store, a blacksmith shop and a grog shop, a few plain houses straggling out to the edge of the forest—such a dreary spectacle was enough to make a traveler pine for the neat comfort of home and more than enough to set the pioneer dreaming of the mansions of the blest in that happier land where the streets are paved with gold." Whitaker, *The Spanish-American Frontier,* p. 11.

13. Turner, *The Frontier in American History,* p. 185.

14. "It is not too much to say that the period of five years following the peace of 1783 was the most critical period in all the history of the American people. The dangers from which we were saved in 1788 were even greater than the dangers from which we were saved in 1865. In the War of Secession the love of union had come to be so strong that thousands of men gave up their lives for it as cheerfully and triumphantly as the martyrs of olden times, who sang hymns of praise even while their flesh was withering in the relentless flames. In 1783 the love of union, as a sentiment for which men would fight, had scarcely come into existence among the people of these states. . . . The length of the [Revolutionary] war and its worst hardships had been chiefly due to want of organization. Congress had steadily declined in power and in respectability; it was much weaker at the end of the war than at the beginning; and there was reason to fear that as soon as the common pressure was removed the need for concerted action would quite cease to be felt, and the scarcely formed Union would break into pieces." Fiske, *The Critical Period,* pp. 56–57.

15. "It would be hazardous, perhaps, to go too far in the direction of accusing Hamilton of having projected the excise for use in whipping the recalcitrant localistic elements of the country into submission to the dominant Federalist ma-

chine. It is hard to escape the conclusion, however, that the excise was the device used by speculators in state securities and by the great property holders in general to shift the burden of 'assumption' to the shoulders of the consumers. At the same time the new nationalistic element, scenting immense profits to be gained by the manipulation of the federal government, and recognizing the states as their chief opponents, took advantage of the opportunity to weaken the latter. These two actions, at least, were deliberate policies and were pushed in spite of very patent public opposition. As Hamilton tersely remarked, he had 'long since learned to hold popular opinion of no value.'" Baldwin, *Whiskey Rebels*, pp. 67–68.

16. *Works*, ed. Jared Sparks, vol. 8, p. 501.

17. "The land speculators . . . were something more than mere real estate agents; or at any rate they were real estate agents cast in a heroic mould. Now they intoxicated a whole Indian tribe, now corrupted a state legislature, now erected a new state when they found none ready to serve their purpose. Although not one of their major projects was successful in the period under consideration, these speculators played a most important part in it, and did something that was much more important than the mere establishment of another colony or two in the already populous Mississippi Valley. They advertised the West and pointed the way not only for later American settlement, but also for the immediate establishment of posts by the jealous Spaniard. They stirred up Western indignation against Spain and Western discontent with the Union, and one of their number, Patrick Henry, very nearly prevented the adoption of the present federal constitution because of his dissatisfaction with the Northern States' attitude towards the development of the Southwest. Finally, it was these speculators who forced the issue of the controversy between their government and Spain, for the success of their speculative schemes depended upon the free

use of the Mississippi." Whitaker, *The Spanish-American Frontier*, pp. 48–49.

18. It is now northwestern Alabama, not far from the city of Florence. The federal government only recently moved to dig a waterway between this place and the upper reaches of the Tombigbee, thus resuscitating Blount's original plan almost two hundred years later.

19. "His greatest gamble, the conspiracy, was in essence purely a business speculation, the greatest of many hundreds such. It failed, the Eastern world castigated him, and he fled to people he knew would understand and applaud." Masterson, *William Blount*, p. 351.

20. "Between the Congress thus constituted and the several state governments the attributes of sovereignty were shared in such a way as to produce a minimum of result with a maximum of effort." Fiske, *American Revolution*, p. 99.

21. At least, he was *probably* a Mohawk; but he might have been an Onondaga; he was an Iroquois, anyway. The late Henry Wadsworth Longfellow seemed to think that he was a Chippewa, which is a long way off.

22. "The whites might be to blame in some cases, and the Indians in others; but under no combination of circumstances was it possible to obtain possession of the country save as the result of war, or of a peace obtained by the fear of war. Any peace which did not surrender the land was sure in the end to be broken by the whites; and a peace which did surrender the land would be broken by the Indians." Roosevelt, *The Winning of the West*, vol. 4, p. 121.

23. A former Boston bookseller, he had been in charge of artillery for the Continental Army. He is credited with being the first to call George Washington "the Father of His Country." Callahan, *Henry Knox*, p. 259. Knoxville, Tennessee, is named for him.

24. Spain had been paying him only $600 a year, but when she learned of this she raised it to $2,000 and a little

later to $3,500. There is no evidence that Good Child King solicited either of these raises, or even took much interest in them. He had all the money he needed.

25. "The Spanish intrigue was the inevitable outcome of the circumstances in which the frontiersmen found themselves. Their hardships—insecurity of life and property—were the universal lot of frontier communities, but it was only human that they should have laid the blame on some human agent. Such an agent they found in the governments of North Carolina and the Confederation. Revolution was in the air, and it would have been surprising had the analogous circumstances of the Westerners not suggested an action similar to that of 1776. To complete the analogy, foreign aid was sought, and the Spanish intrigue was begun." Whitaker, "Spanish Intrigue," *Mississippi Valley Historical Review*, vol. 12, no. 1, p. 173.

"In his desire for personal gain Wilkinson had started the Spanish conspiracy in American history. In fact, he *was* the Spanish conspiracy; while he was active the conspiracy was very much to the fore, and when he was biding his time or engaged elsewhere the conspiracy languished. At intervals in the years that followed the Spanish conspiracy had greater or less vitality and importance as Wilkinson's personal necessities were greater or less. The ambitions and desires of his competitors and opponents were also a factor in keeping the 'conspiracy' alive." Hay and Werner, *The Admirable Trumpeter*, p. 88.

26. The provincial treasurer's report for 1797, a comparatively prosperous year, cotton having become a stable crop upriver, gave the total revenues as 537,869 Spanish dollars, of which 453,064 were in the form of a subsidy from Mexico. Expenditures were 795,662 dollars (Whitaker, *The Mississippi Question*, p. 178). In those days the duty on cotton was $3.25 a bale, but the going price of getting an inspector to look the other way was only 13½¢ a bale (Ibid., p.

134). But there was no cotton when James Wilkinson made his first trip down the Mississippi. It would be several years yet before Eli Whitney of Connecticut invented his world-shaking gin.

27. Much of Wilkinson's life was spent in denying things, most of all any knowledge of even a remote connection with what a churlish world had elected to call the Spanish Conspiracy. In his *Memoirs* (vol. 2, pp. 115–16) he wrote: "But, that I have ever, in all my correspondence and intercourse with the Spanish government, conceded a title of the honour or interests of my country, I most solemnly deny, in the face of God and man; and I have ample and undeniable testimony to shew that I omitted no occasion, to employ my ascendancy over the officers of Spanish Louisiana, to render them subservient to the interest, and accommodation of the United States."

28. *History*, vol. 1, pp. 177–78.

29. It was so spelled, originally, with a small "r," and thought of that way, too. It soon became republican-democratic, a little later democratic-republic, and eventually Democratic, as it still is. It had nothing to do with the present Republican party, as spelled with a capital "R," which, despite its boastful designation of Grand Old Party, or G.O.P., dates only from 1856.

30. Bemis, *Pinckney's Treaty*, pp. 626–31.

31. The reader should be reminded that the Rhine tolls were not abolished until 1804; the Congress of Vienna in 1815 opened many of the rivers in western Europe; and the lower St. Lawrence was not declared free to United States shipping until 1871 (Bemis, *Pinckney's Treaty*, p. 333). Navigation rights to the Volga are still in dispute.

32. Now Memphis, Tennessee.

33. The Constitution as originally framed provided that the man who got the most electoral votes would become President, and the man who got the second most would become Vice-President. The rise of the two-party system had

not then been foretold. Soon after the 1800 tie, Congress and the country passed the twelfth amendment, September 25, 1804, so that such a perilous tangle might not occur again. Alexander Hamilton was not a member of the House, nor of the cabinet, but his voice was strong in Federalist circles. He didn't like either candidate, but he thought that Jefferson was a shade less untrustworthy than Burr, and when neither would make a deal he urged his friends to vote for Jefferson. It could be argued, then—and it has been—that Hamilton single-handedly cost Aaron Burr the Presidency; and that this was one of the reasons why Burr disliked him.

34. "It is not difficult to apportion the credit for this transaction. Napoleon, for reasons having nothing whatever to do with the United States, suddenly determined to get whatever he could for whatever title to Louisiana he had. He threw the province, so to speak, at Livingston, Monroe, Madison, and Jefferson; and they share between them—equally—whatever credit there was in catching and holding it —that is all." Channing, *History*, vol. 4, p. 319 n.

"The very last of his great constructions was the sale of Louisiana. He needed the purchase-money, he selected his purchaser and forced it on him, with a view to upbuilding a giant rival to the gigantic power of Great Britain." Sloane, "The World Aspects of the Louisiana Purchase," *American Historical Review*, vol. 9, 1903–04.

35. It was to be learned, eventually, that the Purchase comprised 875,025 square miles. All the United States east of the Mississippi at that time contained 909,050 square miles.

36. "The annexation of Louisiana was an event so portentous as to defy measurement; it gave a new face to politics, and ranked in historical importance next to the Declaration of Independence and the adoption of the Constitution, events of which it was the logical outcome; but as a matter of diplomacy it was unparalleled, because it cost almost nothing." Adams, *History*, vol. 2, p. 49.

37. This was the present Jackson Square, the heart of the old city, but it was then twice as big as it is now and extended clear to the river.

38. This should have read Hudson. The duel took place on what is now the yards around the West Shore Railroad terminal, not far from the former 42nd Street ferry, which is more than a mile south of the Bergen County line.

39. Syrett and Cooke, *Interview in Weehawken,* p. 157. This, a Wesleyan University Press publication, is easily the best book on the subject. It is the result of collecting and carefully editing all the papers connected with the affair, most of them now in the possession of the New-York Historical Society.

40. The Missouri, perhaps because it had so few islands and had generally flat banks, never was infested with river pirates, who, however, made the lower Mississippi as well as the lower Ohio their own for many years, so that it was risky for any kind of craft to tie up there for the night. It was not until in the winter of 1808–9, when an informal group of neighbors from many miles around wiped out the river-pirate gang at Stack Island, "executing" nineteen men, that the piracy problem could be said to have been solved. The record does not state how the nineteen men were executed, but it is assumed that they were hanged. Stack Island was also known as the Crow's Nest. It was located near the halfway point in a nine-mile reach of river at just about what is now the southeast corner of Arkansas.

41. The present Arkansas-Louisiana line.

42. It was to be one of the causes of the Mexican War of 1846–47. The United States had made, and stuck to, the extraordinary claim that the Louisiana Purchase included all of Texas, its southwestern boundary being the Rio Grande; whereas Mexico, citing the Neutral Ground Treaty, insisted that the boundary was the Sabine.

43. Abernathy, *Burr Conspiracy,* p. 218.

44. He became a major general and was a considerable

figure in the Mexican War. Both Gainesville, Texas, and Gainesville, Florida, where the state university is, were named after him.

45. *History,* vol. 2, pp. 246–47.

46. It is the present western boundary of Florida, the boundary between Florida and Alabama.

47. It is now a part of the state of Louisiana, and has been divided into parishes. It was of military importance at that time because parts of it blocked off Lake Borgne, by means of which New Orleans could conceivably have been attacked from the east.

48. He came back to the United States much later, to practice law for a little while, and to die, at an advanced age, on Staten Island. He is buried, this grandson of Jonathan Edwards, at Princeton, New Jersey. He was a graduate of Princeton, of which his father was the second president.

Bibliography

ABBEY, KATHRYN T. "Efforts of Spain to Maintain Sources of Information in the British Colonies before 1779." *Mississippi Valley Historical Review,* vol. 15, no. 1, pp. 56–68.

———. "Peter Chester's Defense of the Mississippi after the Willing Raid." *Mississippi Valley Historical Review,* vol. 22, no. 1, pp. 17–32.

ABERNATHY, THOMAS PERKINS. *The Burr Conspiracy.* New York: Oxford University Press, 1954.

———. *From Frontier to Plantation in Tennessee: A Study in Frontier Democracy.* Chapel Hill: University of North Carolina Press, 1932.

———. *The South in the New Nation, 1789–1819.* Baton Rouge: Louisiana State University Press, 1961.

ADAMS, CHARLES FRANCIS. *See* ADAMS, JOHN, and ADAMS, JOHN QUINCY.

ADAMS, HENRY. *History of the United States during the Administrations of Thomas Jefferson and James Madison.* 4 vols. New York: Albert and Charles Boni, 1930.

———. *John Randolph.* Boston and New York: Houghton, Mifflin & Co., 1898.

——. *The Life of Albert Gallatin.* New York: Peter Smith, 1943.

ADAMS, HENRY, ed. *Documents Relating to New-England Federalism, 1800–1815.* Boston: Little, Brown and Co., 1905.

ADAMS, HERBERT B. "George Washington's Interest in Western Lands." *Johns Hopkins University Studies in Historical and Political Science,* vol. 3 (1885), pp. 55–77.

ADAMS, JOHN. *Works of John Adams, Second President of the United States.* Edited by Charles Francis Adams. 10 vols. Boston: Little, Brown and Co., 1850–56.

ADAMS, JOHN QUINCY. *Memoirs.* Edited by Charles Francis Adams. 12 vols. Philadelphia: J. B. Lippincott Co., 1874–77.

AITON, ARTHUR S. "The Diplomacy of the Louisiana Cession." *American Historical Review,* vol. 36 (July 1931), pp. 701–20.

ALDEN, GEORGE HENRY. "The State of Franklin." *American Historical Review,* vol. 8 (1902–03), pp. 271–89.

ALDEN, JOHN RICHARD. *The First South.* Baton Rouge: Louisiana State University Press, 1957.

——. *General Gage in America, Being Principally a History of His Role in the American Revolution.* Baton Rouge: Louisiana State University Press, 1948.

ALEXANDER, HOLMES. *Aaron Burr, the Proud Pretender.* New York: Harper & Brothers, 1937.

ALLEN, GARDNER W. *A Naval History of the American Revolution.* 2 vols. Boston: Houghton Mifflin Co., 1913.

ALVORD, CLARENCE WALWORTH. *The Mississippi Valley in British Politics: A Study of the Trade, Land Speculation, and Experiments in Imperialism Culminating in the American Revolution.* 2 vols. Cleveland: Arthur H. Clark Co., 1917.

ANDERSON, JOHN J. *Did the Louisiana Purchase Extend to the Pacific Ocean?* New York: Clark & Maynard, 1881.

BAKELESS, JOHN. *Daniel Boone: Master of the Wilderness.* New York: William Morrow & Co., 1939.

BALDWIN, LELAND D. *The Keelboat Age on Western Waters.* Pittsburgh: University of Pittsburgh Press, 1941.

——. *Whiskey Rebels: The Story of a Frontier Uprising.* Pittsburgh: University of Pittsburgh Press, 1939.

BARBÉ-MARBOIS, FRANÇOIS, MARQUIS DE. *The History of Louisiana, Particularly of the Cession of that Colony to the United*

States of America. Translated by "an American citizen." Philadelphia: Carey and Lea, 1830.

BARNES, EDWARD. *History of the Late War between the United States and Great Britain.* 4 vols. Philadelphia: 1823.

BASSETT, JOHN SPENCER. *The Life of Andrew Jackson.* 2 vols. New York: Doubleday, Page & Co., 1911.

BEIRNE, FRANCIS F. *Shout Treason: The Trial of Aaron Burr.* New York: Hastings House, 1959.

————. *The War of 1812.* New York: E. P. Dutton & Co., Inc., 1949.

BEMIS, SAMUEL FLAGG. *Pinckney's Treaty: A Study of America's Advantage from Europe's Distress, 1783–1800.* Baltimore: Johns Hopkins Press, 1926.

BEVERIDGE, ALBERT J. *The Life of John Marshall.* 2 vols. Boston: Houghton Mifflin Co., 1929.

BILLINGTON, RAY ALLEN. *Westward Expansion: A History of the American Frontier.* New York: Macmillan Co., 1949.

BLAIR, WALTER, and MEINE, FRANKLIN J., eds. *Half Horse, Half Alligator: The Growth of the Mike Fink Legend.* Chicago: University of Chicago Press, 1956.

BODLEY, TEMPLE. *George Rogers Clark: His Life and Public Services.* Boston and New York: Houghton Mifflin Co., 1926.

BOWERS, CLAUDE G. *Jefferson in Power: The Death Struggle of the Federalists.* Boston: Houghton Mifflin Co., 1936.

BOYD, JULIAN P. *See* JEFFERSON, THOMAS.

BRANT, IRVING. *James Madison.* 5 vols. Indianapolis: Bobbs-Merrill Co., 1941–56.

BRETZ, JULIAN P. "Early Land Communication with the Lower Mississippi Valley." *Mississippi Valley Historical Review,* vol. 13, no. 1, pp. 3–29.

BRIDENBAUGH, CARL. *Myths and Realities: Societies of the Colonial South.* Baton Rouge: Louisiana State University Press, 1952.

BROADHEAD, COLONEL JAMES O. "The Louisiana Purchase: Extent of Territory Acquired by the Said Purchase." *Missouri Historical Society Collections,* vol. 1, no. 13.

BROWN, CHARLES RAYMOND. *The Northern Confederacy, According to the Plans of the "Essex Junto," 1769–1814.* Princeton: Princeton University Press, 1915.

BROWN, EVERETT SOMERVILLE. *The Constitutional History of the Louisiana Purchase, 1803–1812.* Berkeley: University of California Press, 1920.

BROWN, STUART GERRY. *The First Republicans: Political Philosophy and Public Policy in the Party of Jefferson and Madison.* Syracuse: Syracuse University Press, 1954.

BURT, A. I. *The United States, Great Britain and British North America from the Revolution to the Establishment of Peace After the War of 1812.* New Haven: Yale University Press, 1940.

CADY, JOHN F. "Western Opinion and the War of 1812." *Ohio Archaeological and Historical Quarterly,* vol. 33 (1924), pp. 427–76.

CALLAHAN, NORTH. *Henry Knox: General Washington's General.* New York and Toronto: Rinehart and Co., Inc., 1958.

CAPERS, GERALD M., JR. *The Biography of a River Town. Memphis: Its Heroic Age.* Chapel Hill: University of North Carolina Press, 1939.

CARR, ALBERT Z. *The Coming of War: An Account of the Remarkable Events Leading to the War of 1812.* Garden City: Doubleday & Co., Inc., 1960.

CARTER, HODDING. *Lower Mississippi.* New York: Farrar & Rinehart, 1942.

CAUGHEY, JOHN WALTON. *Bernardo de Gálvez in Louisiana, 1776–1783.* Berkeley: University of California Press, 1934.

———. *McGillivray of the Creeks.* Norman, Okla.: University of Oklahoma Press, 1938.

———. "The Natchez Rebellion of 1781 and its Aftermath." *Louisiana Historical Quarterly,* vol. 16 (1933), pp. 57–83.

———. "Willing's Expedition down the Mississippi, 1778." *Louisiana Historical Quarterly,* vol. 15, no. 1, pp. 5–36.

CHAMBERS, HENRY E. "West Florida in its Relation to the Historical Cartography of the United States." *Johns Hopkins University Studies in Historical and Political Science,* series 16, no. 5.

CHANNING, EDWARD. *A History of the United States.* 6 vols. New York: Macmillian Co., 1926.

CHARLES, JOSEPH. *The Origins of the American Party System.*

Williamsburg, Va.: Institute of Early American History and Culture, 1956.

CLARK, DANIEL. *Proofs of the Corruption of General James Wilkinson.* Philadelphia: Wm. Hall, Jun., & Geo. W. Pierie, 1809.

COATES, ROBERT M. *The Outlaw Years: The History of the Pirates of the Natchez Trace.* New York: Literary Guild of America, 1930.

COLEMAN, CHRISTOPHER S. "The Ohio Valley in the Preliminaries of the War of 1812." *Mississippi Valley Historical Review,* vol. 7, pp. 39–50.

COOKE, JEAN G. *See* SYRETT, HAROLD C.

CORKRAN, DAVID H. *The Cherokee Frontier: Conflict and Survival, 1740–1762.* Norman, Okla.: University of Oklahoma Press, 1962.

COX, ISAAC JOSLIN. "The Border Missions of General George Mathews." *Mississippi Valley Historical Review,* vol. 12, no. 3, pp. 309–33.

———. "General Wilkinson and His Later Intrigues with the Spaniards." *American Historical Review,* vol. 19, pp. 794–812.

———. *The West Florida Controversy, 1798–1813: A Study in American Diplomacy.* Baltimore: Johns Hopkins Press, 1918.

CRAMER, ZADOK. *The Navigator; Containing Directors For Navigating The Monongahela, Allegheny, Ohio and Mississippi Rivers.* Ann Arbor, Mich.: University Microfilms, Inc., 1966.

CRANE, VERNER W. *The Southern Frontier, 1670–1732.* Durham, N.C.: Duke University Press, 1928.

CRESSWELL, NICHOLAS. *Journal.* New York: Dial Press, 1928.

CUSHMAN, H. B. *History of the Choctaw, Chickasaw and Natchez Indians.* Greenville, Tex.: Headlight Printing House, 1899.

DAVIS, MATTHEW LIVINGSTON. *Memoirs of Aaron Burr.* 2 vols. New York: Harper & Brothers, 1836–37.

DAVIS, MAJOR P. M. *An Official and Full Detail of the Great Battle of New Orleans.* New York, 1836.

DEBO, ANGIE. *The Rise and Fall of the Chocktaw Republic.* Norman, Okla.: University of Oklahoma Press, 1934.

DORSEY, FLORENCE L. *Master of the Mississippi.* Boston: Houghton Mifflin Co., 1941.

DWIGHT, THEODORE. *History of the Hartford Convention.* New

York: N. & J. White; Boston: Russell, Odiorne & Co., 1833.

ESPOSITO, COLONEL VINCENT J., ed. *The West Point Atlas of American Wars*. 2 vols. New York: Frederick A. Praeger, 1959.

FARRAND, MAX. "The Commercial Privileges of the Treaty of 1803." *American Historical Review*, vol. 7, no. 3.

FISKE, JOHN. *The Critical Period of American History*. Boston and New York: Houghton, Mifflin and Co., 1898.

FITZPATRICK, JOHN C. *See* WASHINGTON, GEORGE.

FOREMAN, GRANT. "River Navigation in the Early Southwest." *Mississippi Valley Historical Review*, vol. 15, no. 1, pp. 34–55.

FORTIER, ALCÉE. *A History of Louisiana*. New York: Goupil & Co., 1904.

FULLER, H. B. *The Purchase of Florida: Its History and Diplomacy*. Cleveland, 1906.

GANOE, WILLIAM ADDLEMAN. *The History of the United States Army*. New York and London: D. Appleton-Century Co., 1943.

GAYARRE, CHARLES E. A. *History of Louisiana*. 4 vols. New York: William J. Widdleton, 1866.

GEER, CURTIS MANNING. *The Louisiana Purchase and the Westward Movement*. Philadelphia: G. Barrie & Sons, 1904.

GLEIG, GEORGE ROBERT. *A Narrative of the Campaigns of the British Arms at Washington and New Orleans, under General Ross, Pakenham and Lambert, in the Years 1814 and 1815*. London: John Murray, 1921.

GOODMAN, WARREN H. "The Origins of the War of 1812: a Survey of Changing Interpretations." *Mississippi Valley Historical Review*, vol. 28, no. 2.

GREENE, EVARTS B., and HARRINGTON, VIRGINIA D. *American Population before the Federal Census of 1790*. New York: Columbia University Press, 1932.

HACKER, LOUIS M. "Western Land Hunger and the War of 1812: A Conjecture." *Mississippi Valley Historical Review*, vol. 10 (March 1924), pp. 365–95.

HAGGARD, JUAN VILLASANA. *The Neutral Ground between Louisiana and Texas*. Austin: University of Texas, 1942.

HARRINGTON, VIRGINIA D. *See* GREENE, EVARTS B.

HASKINS, DR. CHARLES H. "The Yazoo Land Companies." *Papers* of the American Historical Association, vol. 5 (1891), pp. 395–437.

HAY, THOMAS ROBSON, and WERNER, M. R. *The Admirable Trumpeter: A Biography of General James Wilkinson.* Garden City: Doubleday, Doran & Co., 1941.

HEADLEY, JOEL TYLER. *The Second War with England.* 2 vols. New York: Charles Scribner's Sons, 1953.

HEMPHILL, W. EDWIN. "The Jeffersonian Background of the Louisiana Purchase." *Mississippi Valley Historical Review,* vol. 22, no. 1, pp. 17–32.

HENDERSON, ARCHIBALD. *The Conquest of the Old Southwest: The Romantic Story of the Early Pioneers into Virginia, the Carolinas, Tennessee, and Kentucky, 1740–1790.* New York: Century Co., 1920.

HERMANN, BINGER. *The Louisiana Purchase and Our Title West of the Rocky Mountains.* Washington, D. C.: Government Printing Office, 1900.

HINSDALE, B. A. "Establishment of the First Southern Boundary of the United States." *Annual Report of the American Historical Association for 1893.* Washington, D. C.: Government Printing Office, 1894.

HOSMER, JAMES K. *The History of the Louisiana Purchase.* New York: D. Appleton and Co., 1902.

HOUCH, LOUIS. *The Boundaries of the Louisiana Purchase.* St. Louis: P. Roeder, 1901.

HOWARD, C. N. *The British Development of West Florida, 1763–69.* Berkeley: University of California Press, 1947.

HYDE, H. MONTGOMERY. *The Amazing Story of John Law: The History of an Honest Adventurer.* Amsterdam: Home & Van Thal, 1948.

JACOBS, JAMES RIPLEY. *The Beginning of the U. S. Army, 1783–1812.* Princeton: Princeton University Press, 1947.

———. *Tarnished Warrior: Major-General James Wilkinson.* New York: Macmillan Co., 1938.

JAMES, D. CLAYTON. *Antebellum Natchez.* Baton Rouge: Louisiana State University Press, 1968.

JAMES, JAMES ALTON. *The Life of George Rogers Clark.* Chicago: University of Chicago Press, 1928.

———. "Spanish Influence in the West during the American Revolution." *Mississippi Valley Historical Review,* vol. 4 (1917), pp. 193–208.

JAMES, WILLIAM. *A Full and Correct Account of the Military Occurences of the Late War between Great Britain and the United States of America.* 2 vols. London: Printed for the author, 1818.

JEFFERSON, THOMAS. *The Papers of Thomas Jefferson.* Edited by Julian P. Boyd. 13 vols. Princeton: Princeton University Press, 1950.

———. *The Writings of Thomas Jefferson.* Edited by Andrew A. Lipscomb. 20 vols. Washington, D. C.: The Thomas Jefferson Memorial Association, 1903.

JENKINSON, ISAAC. *Aaron Burr, His Personal and Political Relations with Thomas Jefferson and Alexander Hamilton.* Richmond, Ind.: M. Cullaton & Co., 1902.

JENSEN, MERRILL. *The Articles of Confederation: An Interpretation of the Social-Constitutional History of the American Nation, 1774–1781.* Madison: University of Wisconsin Press, 1940.

JOHNSON, CECIL. *British West Florida, 1763–1783.* New Haven: Yale University Press, 1943.

JOHNSON, CHARLES BURR. *The True Aaron Burr: A Biographical Sketch.* New York: A. S. Barnes & Co., 1902.

KAPLAN, LAWRENCE S. *Jefferson and France: An Essay on Politics and Political Ideas.* New Haven: Yale University Press, 1967.

KELLOGG, LOUISE PHELPS. *See* THWAITES, REUBEN GOLD.

KINNAIRD, LAWRENCE, ed. "Spain in the Mississippi Valley, 1765–1794." 3 vols. *Annual Report of the American Historical Association for the Year 1945.* Washington, D. C.: Government Printing Office, 1946.

KNAPP, SAMUEL L. *The Life of Aaron Burr.* New York: Wiley & Long, 1835.

KOCH, ADRIENNE. *Jefferson and Madison: The Great Collaboration.* New York: Alfred A. Knopf, Inc., 1950.

LABAREE, LEONARD W. *Royal Government in America: A Study of the British Colonial System before 1783.* New York: Frederick Ungar Publishing Co., 1958.

LANGFORD, NATHANIEL PITT. "The Louisiana Purchase and Pre-

ceding Spanish Intrigues for Dismemberment of the Union."
Minnesota Historical Society Collections, vol. 9.

LYON, E. WILSON. *Louisiana in French Diplomacy, 1759–1804*.
Norman, Okla.: University of Oklahoma Press, 1934.

———. *The Man Who Sold Louisiana: The Career of François
Barbé-Marbois*. Norman, Okla.: University of Oklahoma Press,
1942.

McCALEB, WALTER FLAVIUS. *The Aaron Burr Conspiracy and A
New Light on Aaron Burr*. New York: Argosy-Antiquarian,
Ltd., 1966.

McELROY, ROBERT McNUTT. *Kentucky in the Nation's History*.
New York: Moffat, Yard and Co., 1909.

McLEMORE, R. A. "Jeffersonian Diplomacy in the Purchase of
Louisiana, 1803." *Louisiana Historical Quarterly*, vol. 18
(1935), pp. 346–53.

McMASTER, JOHN BACH. *A History of the People of the United
States, from the Revolution to the Civil War*. 8 vols. New
York: D. Appleton and Co., 1892.

MAIN, JACKSON TURNER. *The Antifederalists: Critics of the Constitution, 1781–1788*. Chapel Hill: University of North Carolina
Press, 1961.

MALONE, HENRY THOMPSON. *Cherokees of the Old South: A People
in Transition*. Athens, Ga.: University of Georgia Press, 1956.

MARSHALL, THOMAS MAITLAND. *A History of the Western Boundary of the Louisiana Purchase, 1819–1841*. Berkeley: University of California Press, 1914.

MARTELL, J. S. "A Side Light on Federalist Strategy." *American
Historical Review*, vol. 43, pp. 553–66.

MASTERSON, WILLIAM H. *William Blount*. Baton Rouge: Louisiana
State University Press, 1954.

MEINE, FRANKLIN J. *See* BLAIR, WALTER.

MORISON, SAMUEL ELIOT. *Life and Letters of Harrison Gray Otis,
1765–1848*. 2 vols. Boston: Houghton Mifflin Co., 1913.

MORRIS, RICHARD B. *The Peacemakers: The Great Powers and
American Independence*. New York: Harper & Row, 1965.

OGG, FREDERIC AUSTIN. *The Opening of the Mississippi: A Struggle
for Supremacy in the American Interior*. New York: Macmillan
Co., 1904.

OLIVER, FREDERICK SCOTT. *Alexander Hamilton: An Essay on American Union.* New York: G. P. Putnam's Sons, 1907.

PARSONS, EDWARD ALEXANDER. "The Letters of Robert R. Livingston: The Diplomatic Story of the Louisiana Purchase." *Proceedings of the American Antiquarian Society.* New series, vol. 52, pp. 363–407.

PARTON, JAMES. *The Life and Times of Aaron Burr.* New York: Mason Brothers, 1858.

———. *The Life of Andrew Jackson.* 3 vols. New York: Mason Brothers, 1860.

PATRICK, REMBERT W. *Florida Fiasco: Rampant Rebels on the Georgia-Florida Border, 1810–1815.* Athens, Ga.: University of Georgia Press, 1954.

PAULLIN, CHARLES OSCAR. *The Navy of the American Revolution: Its Administration, Its Policy, and Its Achievements.* Cleveland: Burrows Brothers Co., 1906.

PAXSON, FREDERIC. *History of the American Frontier, 1763–1893.* Boston: Houghton Mifflin Co., 1924.

PEASE, THEODORE C. "The Mississippi Boundary of 1763: A Reappraisal of Responsibility." *American Historical Review,* vol. 40 (1935), p. 278.

PELLEW, GEORGE. *John Jay.* Boston: Houghton, Mifflin & Co., 1890.

PHILBRICK, FRANCIS S. *The Rise of the West, 1754–1830.* New York: Harper & Row, 1965.

PICKERING, OCTAVUS, and UPHAM, CHARLES WENTWORTH. *The Life of Timothy Pickering.* 4 vols. Boston: Little, Brown & Co., 1867–73.

POAGE, GEORGE RAWLINGS. *Henry Clay and the Whig Party.* Chapel Hill: University of North Carolina Press, 1936.

PRATT, JULIUS W. *Expansionists of 1812.* New York: Macmillan Co., 1925.

———. "Western Aims in the War of 1812." *Mississippi Valley Historical Review,* vol. 12, no. 1, pp. 36–50.

QUINCY, JOSIAH P. "The Louisiana Purchase; and the Appeal to Posterity." *Proceedings of the Massachusetts Historical Society.* Second series, vol. 18 (1903), pp. 48–59.

RIEGEL, ROBERT E. *America Moves West.* New York: Henry Holt and Co., 1930.

RIVES, GEORGE L. "Spain and the United States in 1795." *American*

Historical Review, vol. 4 (October 1898), pp. 62–79.

ROBERTSON, REVEREND CHARLES FRANKLIN. "The Attempts to Separate the West from the American Union." *Missouri Historical Society Collections,* vol. I, no. 10.

———. "The Louisiana Purchase in Its Influence upon the American System." *Papers of the American Historical Association,* vol. I, no. 4.

ROBERTSON, JAMES ALEXANDER. *Louisiana under the Rule of Spain, France, and the United States, 1785–1807.* 2 vols. Cleveland, Ohio: Arthur H. Clark Co., 1911.

ROOSEVELT, THEODORE. *The Winning of the West.* 4 vols. New York: G. P. Putnam's Sons, 1900.

ROTHERT, OTTO A. *The Outlaws of Cave-in-Rock: Historical Accounts of the Famous Highwaymen and River Pirates Who Operated in Pioneer Days upon the Ohio and Mississippi Rivers and Over the Old Natchez Trace.* Cleveland, Ohio: Arthur H. Clark Co., 1924.

ROWLAND, MRS. DUNBAR. *Andrew Jackson's Campaign against the British, or, The Mississippi Territory in the War of 1812.* New York: Macmillan Co., 1926.

———. "Marking the Natchez Trace: An Historic Highway of the Lower South." *Publications of the Mississippi Historical Society,* vol. 11. University, Miss.: Mississippi Historical Society, 1910.

RUSSELL, CARL P. *Guns on the Early Frontiers: A History of Firearms from Colonial Times through the Years of the Western Fur Trade.* Berkeley and Los Angeles: University of California Press, 1957.

SCHACHNER, NATHAN. *Aaron Burr, a Biography.* New York: Frederick A. Stokes Co., 1937.

———. *Alexander Hamilton, a Biography.* D. Appleton-Century Co., 1946.

———. *Thomas Jefferson: a Biography.* 2 vols. New York: D. Appleton-Century-Crofts, Inc., 1951.

SCHOULER, JAMES. *History of the United States of America under the Constitution.* 8 vols. New York: Dodd, Mead & Co., 1892.

SCHURZ, CARL. *Life of Henry Clay.* 2 vols. Boston: Houghton, Mifflin & Co., 1887.

SHEPHERD, WILLIAM R. "Wilkinson and the Beginnings of the

Spanish Conspiracy." *American Historical Review,* vol. 9, pp. 490–506.

SHREVE, ROYAL ORNAN. *The Finished Scoundrel: General James Wilkinson.* Indianapolis: Bobbs-Merrill Co., 1933.

SINCLAIR, HAROLD. *The Port of New Orleans.* Garden City: Doubleday & Co., 1942.

SLOANE, WILLIAM M. "Napoleon's Plans for a Colonial System." *American Historical Review,* vol. 4 (April 1899), pp. 439–55.

———. "The World Aspects of the Louisiana Purchase." *American Historical Review,* vol. 9 (1903–04), pp. 507–21.

SMITH, FRANK E. *The Yazoo River.* New York: Rinehart & Co., Inc., 1954.

SMITH, THEODORE CLARK. "War Guilt in 1812." *Massachusetts Historical Society Proceedings,* vol. 64 (1931), pp. 319–45.

STEVENS, WILLIAM OLIVER. *Pistols at Ten Paces: the Story of the Code of Honor in America.* Boston: Houghton Mifflin Co., 1949.

SYRETT, HAROLD C., and COOKE, JEAN G., eds. *Interview in Wee-hawken: The Burr-Hamilton Duel, As Told in the Original Documents.* With an introduction and conclusion by Willard M. Wallace. Middletown, Conn.: Wesleyan University Press, 1960.

TAYLOR, G. R. "Agrarian Discontent in the Mississippi Valley Preceding the War of 1812." *Mississippi Valley Historical Review,* vol. 10.

———. "Colonial Settlement and Early Revolutionary Activity in West Florida up to 1779." *Mississippi Valley Historical Review,* vol. 22, no. 3, pp. 351–60.

THOMAS, DAVID YANCEY. *A History of Military Government in Newly Acquired Territory of the United States.* New York: Columbia University Press, 1904.

THWAITES, REUBEN GOLD. *Daniel Boone.* New York and London: D. Appleton and Co., 1931.

———, and KELLOGG, LOUISE PHELPS. *Frontier Defense of the Upper Ohio, 1777–1778.* Madison: Wisconsin Historical Society, 1912.

TURNER, FREDERICK JACKSON. "The Diplomatic Contest for the Mississippi Valley." *Atlantic Monthly,* vol. 93 (1904), pp. 676–91 and 807–17.

————. "Documents on the Blount Conspiracy, 1795–1797." *American Historical Review*, vol. X, pp. 574–606.

————. *The Frontier in American History*. New York: Henry Holt and Co., 1920.

————. "The Origin of Genêt's Projected Attack on Louisiana and the Floridas." *American Historical Review*, vol. 3, pp. 650–71.

————. "The Policy of France toward the Mississippi Valley in the Period of Washington and Adams." *American Historical Review*, vol. 10, pp. 249–79.

————. "Western State-Making in the Revolutionary Era." *American Historical Review*, vol. 1, nos. 1 and 2, 1895–96.

UPDYKE, FRANK A. *The Diplomacy of the War of 1812*. Baltimore: Johns Hopkins Press, 1915.

UPHAM, CHARLES WENTWORTH. *See* PICKERING, OCTAVUS.

VAN EVERY, DALE. *A Company of Heroes: The American Frontier*. New York: William Morrow and Co., 1962.

VAN TYNE, CHARLES H. "Why Did We Fight in 1812? The Causes and Significance of Our Last War with Great Britain." *Independent*, vol. 74 (1913), pp. 1327–31.

WALKER, ALEXANDER. *The Life of Andrew Jackson, to Which is Added an Authentic Narrative of the Memorable Achievements of the Army at New Orleans, in the Winter of 1814–15*. Philadelphia: G. G. Evans, 1860.

WALLACE, WILLARD M. *See* SYRETT, HAROLD C. and COOKE, JEAN G.

WARD, JOHN WILLIAM. *Andrew Jackson, Symbol for an Age*. New York: Oxford University Press, 1955.

WARFIELD, ETHELBERT D. "The Constitutional Aspects of Kentucky's Struggle for Autonomy—1784–92." *Papers of the American Historical Association*, vol. 4, part 1, October 1891.

WASHINGTON, GEORGE. *The Writings of George Washington, from the Original Manuscript Sources, 1745–1799*. Edited by John C. Fitzpatrick. 39 vols. Washington, D. C.: Government Printing Office, 1931–44.

WEBSTER, SIDNEY. *Two Treaties of Paris and the Supreme Court*. New York and London: Harper & Brothers, 1901.

WEINBERG, ALBERT K. *Manifest Destiny: a Study of Nationalist Expansion in American History*. Baltimore: Johns Hopkins University Press, 1935.

WERNER, M. R. *See* HAY, THOMAS ROBSON.

WHITAKER, ARTHUR PRESTON. "Harry Innes and the Spanish Intrigue: 1794–1795." *Mississippi Valley Historical Review*, vol. 15, no. 2, pp. 236–48.

———. *The Mississippi Question, 1795–1803: A Study in Trade, Politics, and Diplomacy*. New York and London: D. Appleton-Century Co., 1934.

———. "The Muscle Shoals Speculation, 1783–1789." *Mississippi Valley Historical Review*, vol. 13, no. 1, pp. 365–86.

———. "New Light on the Treaty of San Lorenzo." *Mississippi Valley Historical Review*, vol. 15, no. 4, pp. 435–54.

———. "Spanish Intrigue in the Old Southwest: An Episode, 1788–89." *Mississippi Valley Historical Review*, vol. 12, no. 1, pp. 155–76.

———. *The Spanish-American Frontier: 1783–1795. The Westward Movement and the Spanish Retreat in the Mississippi Valley*. Boston: Houghton Mifflin Co., 1927.

WILKINSON, JAMES. *Memoirs of My Own Times*. 3 vols. Philadelphia: Abraham Small, 1816.

WILLIAMS, SAMUEL COLE. *History of the Lost State of Franklin*. Johnson City, Tenn.: Watauga Press, 1924.

WINSOR, JUSTIN. *The Colonies and the Republic West of the Alleghanies, 1763–1798*. Boston: Houghton, Mifflin & Co., 1897.

———. *The Struggle in America between England and France, 1697–1763*. Boston: Houghton, Mifflin & Co., 1895.

WOOLERY, WILLIAM K. "The Relation of Thomas Jefferson to American Foreign Policy, 1783–1795." *Johns Hopkins Studies in Historical and Political Science*, vol. 45 (1927), pp. 83–84.

Index

A

Adams, Abigail, 47
Adams, Henry, 82, 83, 181
Adams, John, 47, 81, 85, 87, 111, 113
Adams, John Quincy, 145
Adams, Samuel, 80
Alcudia, Duke of. *See* Godoy
Allouez, Father Claude, 11
Alston, Aaron Burr, 171
Alston, John, 169
Alston, Theodosia Burr, 161, 169
Amis, Thomas, 40, 76
Arnold, Benedict, 73, 74

B

Barbé-Marbois, François, Marquis de, 135, 136, 140
Bastrop, Baron de, 170
Blennerhassett, Harman, 171, 178
Blount, William, 46, 47, 65, 72, 76; note 18; note 19
Bonaparte, Joseph, 137
Bonaparte, Lucien, 137
Bonaparte, Napoleon, 115–16, 132–35, 137–38, 140, 146, 160, 186

Bonaparte, Pauline, 133
Boone, Daniel, 22, 24, 142, 143
Bowles, William Augustus, 69, 72
Bradford, Gamaliel, 73
Burr, Aaron, 71, 114; duel with Hamilton, 151–59; Western activities, 160, 162–64, 166–67, 169, 170–77; note 33; note 48

C

Cabot, George, 194
Cameron, Alexander, 65
Carlos III of Spain, 12, 39, 94; note 4
Carlos IV of Spain, 94, 95, 104, 105
Carolina, gunboat, 198
Carondelet, Baron de, 102, 103
Caso Yrujo, Marquis de, 126, 146
Chisholm, John, 65
Church, John Barker, 156
Claiborne, Governor William Charles Coles, 148, 175, 183
Clark, Daniel, 160
Clark, George Rogers, 3, 5, 14, 15, 41, 92, 93, 103; note 8
Clark, Captain John, 24, 142

Clay, Henry, 51–53
Clinton, Governor DeWitt, 158
Cochrane, Vice Admiral Sir
    Alexander, 187, 198
Colbert, James, 63, 64
Cramer, Zadok, note 1
Crazy Horse, 66
Crockett, Davy, 22

D

Daveiss, Joseph Hamilton, 172
De la Croix, Dussau, 195
de Soto, Hernando, 11, 12
Dunmore, Lord, 69

E

Ellicott, Andrew, 105, 106, 107
Embuscade, L', frigate, 89

F

Ferguson, Kenneth, 65
Fergusson, Captain John, 7, 8,
    9
Fink, Mike, 120, 121, 123
Floyd, Davis, 178
Fluger, Colonel, 166
Fluger, "Pluggy," 166
Forbes, John, 65
Foster, Stephen Collins, 47, 48
Fox, Charles James, 168
Franklin, Benjamin, 45, 85, 99,
    111, 180
Fraser, Alexander, 65
Frederick the Great, 116

Freeman, Thomas, 107

G

Gage, Lieutenant General Wil-
    liam, 13
Gaines, Edmund Pendleton,
    178; note 44
Galloway, Joseph, 75
Gálvez, Governor Bernardo de,
    7, 8, 9, 14, 15, 16, 17, 18, 19,
    38, 68, 181; note 5; note 9
Gálvez, José de, 8
Gardoqui, Diego de, 39, 40
Garrard, Governor, 126, 127
Gates, Major General Horatio,
    74
Gayoso de Lemos, Manuel, 102,
    103, 105, 106, 107
Genêt, Edmond Charles, 87–
    89, 91–93, 103
Gérard, Conrad Alexandre, 89
Geronimo, 66
Gibbs, Major General Sir Sam-
    uel, 202
Girty, James, 63
Girty, Simon, 63
Godoy, Don Manuel Luis de,
    95, 96, 100, 101, 131, 146,
    180
Gorges, Sir Ferdinando, 144
Grasse, François Joseph Paul,
    Comte de, 19
Greene, Major General Na-
    thanael, 118
Griswold, Gaylord, 148
Gustavus Adolphus, king of
    Sweden, 115

H

Hamilton, Alexander, 34, 36–37, 42, 87–88, 91, 96, 98, 103; duel with Burr, 151–156; note 15; note 33
Hanna, Reverend, 107
Harpe, Micajah ("Big"), 164–67
Harpe, Wiley ("Little"), 164–67
Henry, Patrick, 15, 45, 80, 183; note 17
Hiawatha, 54; note 21
Hill, Lieutenant General Lord, 187
Hosack, Dr. David, 151, 154
Hutchins, Anthony, 5

I

Innes, Judge Harry, 80
Irving, Washington, 184

J

Jackson, Andrew, 159, 166, 187–88, 190–93, 195–96
Jay, John, 39, 40, 41, 96–99, 101
Jefferson, Thomas, 36, 57, 82, 86, 88, 96, 100, 109, 111–15, 127, 144–45, 173, 175, 180–82; note 33
Jones, Lieutenant Thomas ap Catesby, 191

K

Keane, Major General John, 195, 202

Knox, Henry, 36, 70, 71, 87; note 23

L

Lafayette, Major General Marie Joseph Paul Yves Roch Gilbert du Motier, Marquis de, 19
Lafitte, Jean, 190
Lafitte, Pierre, 190
Lambert, Major General John, 202
Law, John, 43–45, 64, 118
Leclerc, General Charles Victor Emmanuel, 133
Lee, Major General Charles, 14, 15
Leon, Ponce de, 12
Leslie, John, 65
Lewis, Captain Meriwether, 24, 142
Livingston, Robert R., 128, 130, 132, 134–38, 140, 143, 145, 181, 182
Louis XIV of France, 38, 43, 109
Louis XV of France, 43; note 4
Louisiana, gunboat, 198
L'Ouverture, Toussaint. *See* Toussaint L'Ouverture
Luzerne, Chevalier Anne-César de la, 89
Lynch, Charles, 170

M

McGillivray, Alexander, 49, 66–69, 70–72, 109

McGillivray, Lachlan, 67
MacIntosh, William, 65
Madison, James, 114, 145, 182, 187, 195
Marlborough, duke of, 115–16
Marquette, Père, 11
Marshall, Chief Justice John, 178
Mason, James, 163–64, 167
Mason, Marguerite Douglas, 163
Merry, Anthony, 168
Miranda, Francisco, 169
Miró, Governor Estevan, 68
Monroe, James, 127–28, 130, 135, 137–38, 140, 143, 145, 153–54, 181–82, 191–92
Morales, Don Juan Ventura, 125–26
Morris, Robert, 1

N

Navarro, Don Martin, 68
Nicholas, Wilson Cary, 145
Nolan, Philip, 81

O

O'Reilly, Alexander, 4, 13, 17; note 2
Owens, Henry, 80

P

Pakenham, Major General Sir Edward, 187, 195, 198–99, 202

Panton, William, 65, 68, 72
Pendleton, Nathaniel, 151–52, 156
Penn, William, 144
Pickles, Captain William, 17
Pinckney, Thomas, 96, 97, 99, 100, 101
Pineda, Alvarez de, 11, 12
Pitt, William, earl of Chatham, 2
Pitt, the younger, 168
Pollock, Oliver, 3, 4, 6, 9, 14, 15, 16
Pontiac, 56, 66, 76
Pope, Lieutenant "Crazy," 106, 107
Power, Thomas, 81, 104

Q

Quincy, Josiah, 183

R

Randolph, Edmund, 87
Randolph, John, 51–53
Rattletrap, gunboat, 2, 5, 7
Rebecca, gunboat, 7, 17
Reynolds, Mrs. Maria, 153
Rice, Sally, 165
Rillieux, Vizente, 17
Roberts, Betsey, 165
Roberts, Susan, 165
Rochambeau, General Jean Baptiste, 19, 34
Rochambeau, General Donatien Marie Joseph, 134

Roosevelt, Theodore, 73
Ross, Senator James, 127
Ross, Major General Robert, 187

S

Salcedo, Governor Juan de, 125
Sevier, Governor John ("Nollichucky Jack"), 32
Shays, Daniel, 32
Sitting Bull, 66
Sylph, H.M.S., frigate, 7

T

Talleyrand-Périgord, Maurice de, 116, 128, 130, 132, 135, 137, 140
Tecumseh, 66
Thornton, Colonel William, 195, 199
Toussaint L'Ouverture, 133
Twain, Mark, 34
Tyler, Comfort, 178

U

Unzaga y Amézaga, Governor Luis de, 13, 14

V

Van Ness, William P., 151, 152, 156
Villeré, Gabriel, 193, 195

W

Washington, George, 34, 36, 41–42, 45, 47, 57–58, 70–71, 74, 81, 87–88, 89, 91, 96, 98, 184
Wayne General Anthony, 58, 70, 82
Whitney, Eli, 118; note 36
Wilkinson, General James, 51, 73–78, 79, 80–83, 103–4, 150, 159, 160, 167, 169, 173–78, 184–85; note 25; note 27
Willing, James, 1–10, 15; note 1; note 3
Willing, Thomas, 1